S0-BCL-873

The Taming of the Shrew

by William Shakespeare

Perfection Learning® Corporation
Logan, Iowa 51546-0500

Editorial Director	Julie A. Schumacher
Senior Editor	Rebecca Christian
Series Editor	Rebecca Burke
Editorial Assistant	Kate Winzenburg
Writer, Modern Version	Beth Obermiller
Design Director	Randy Messer
Design	Mark Hagenberg
Production	PerfecType
Art Research	Laura Wells
Cover Art	Brad Holland

© 2004 **Perfection Learning® Corporation**
1000 North Second Avenue, P.O. Box 500
Logan, Iowa 51546-0500
Tel: 1-800-831-4190 • Fax: 1-800-543-2745

All rights reserved. No part of this book may be reproduced, stored in a retrieval system, or transmitted in any form or by any means, electronic, mechanical, photocopying, recording, or otherwise, without prior permission of the publisher.

Printed in the United States of America.

Paperback ISBN 0-7891-6086-2
Cover Craft ISBN 0-7569-1488-4
10 11 12 13 PP 18 17 16

Table of Contents

The Taming of the Shrew
A Matter of Interpretation

Like all of Shakespeare's plays, *The Taming of the Shrew* is ripe for interpretation. Everyone—not just Shakespearean scholars—can form an opinion about Shakespeare's real intentions in creating this famous battle between the sexes. Does he truly believe that willful, bossy Kate is "tamed" by the ranting and ravings of her husband, Petruchio, by play's end? Or does she just seem to submit, while saying nothing that cannot be interpreted another way?

Evidence abounds that Shakespeare considers Kate well and truly tamed. And in times past, many young girls stitched needlework samplers with these instructive words from Kate's last speech:

> Such duty as the subject owes the prince,
> Even such a woman oweth to her husband;
> And when she is froward, peevish, sullen, sour,
> And not obedient to his honest will,
> What is she but a foul contending rebel,
> And graceless traitor to her loving lord? (Act V, Scene ii)

We must keep in mind, however, that Kate is an actor playing a part in a play within a play—one put on by a mischievous lord to fool a

Petruchio forces Katherine to leave her wedding, painted by Francis Wheatley, published 1795.

drunken tinker (named Christopher Sly). How seriously do we take the words of a male actor (as actors were in Shakespeare's day) playing the part of a woman in a comic play? Especially one that is put on as a practical joke! It would seem wise not to take the words of Kate's famous "submission" speech *too* seriously.

How to Be a Woman

In Shakespeare's day, most women who received schooling were taught only basic reading and writing. In *The Taming of the Shrew*, Baptista—a man of nobility—is typical of the upper class in hiring a tutor for his daughters, Kate and Bianca. Queen Elizabeth—the most famous "graduate" of this sort of education for young wealthy women—was renowned for her mastery of foreign languages and had also studied math, history, and other subjects from a young age. But noble women who were *not* heads of state were schooled mostly for social refinement, not so they could pursue practical professions in the law, medicine, education, or business.

And there were many Elizabethans who felt that even this degree of schooling was unnatural. Shakespearean dramatists and scholars Joseph Papp and Elizabeth Kirkland report in their work on Elizabethans that "one writer compared a woman with an education to a madman with a sword: You just couldn't tell what she'd do with it!"

In the Elizabethan age, upper-class women who married were likely to spend their free time "writing letters, singing, dancing, strolling in the garden, playing with dainty little pet dogs, and poring over needlework," according to Papp and Kirkland. While their domestic staffs took care of the cooking, cleaning, and child-rearing details, these women studied the Bible and other religious texts and made themselves good companions for their spouses.

The Elizabethans believed that the family was a little world that mirrored the bigger world, the one ruled by the State and Church. Just as the husband was the ultimate authority over his wife and children, the king and queen and clergy had iron rule over their subjects. Petruchio's confident assertion of power over Kate after their marriage—"I will be master of what is mine own. / She is my goods,

© George E. Joseph

Tracey Ullman as Kate and Morgan Freeman as Petruchio in a production with a western theme, Delacorte Theatre, 1990

Grumio and Petruchio

my chattels; she is my house, / My household stuff, my field, my barn . . ."—would not have been quite as shocking to an Elizabethan audience as it must be to contemporary ears.

Along with being subjected to her husband's authority, a woman entering marriage had no choice but to take her husband's last name and his rank. Upon *her* death, he would inherit all her lands; upon *his* death, she would legally acquire only one third of his.

Standards for a woman's conduct and character were uncompromising: She should not be talkative, assertive, or in any other way immodest. The physical ideal was also rigidly held: She should be fair-skinned, soft, and round-figured. The "natural" order of things was rarely contested; a wife did not question her husband's rule over her. Consequences of "shrewish" behavior ranged from name-calling and being shunned to public humiliation and even torture. Almost everyone in Elizabethan society agreed (publicly, anyway) that women like Kate needed to be tamed as much as did Petruchio's wild falcons. Some women fought back—with pamphlets and similar small-scale protests—but they were in the minority. In early modern times, men held most of the power—social, legal, and religious—leaving women little freedom to mount successful protests.

Sources and Theatrical History

The Taming of the Shrew was published in Shakespeare's First Folio (his first published collection of plays) in 1623. Scholars believe it is one of the playwright's earlier plays, probably written before 1594. Unlike many of his other plays, this one does not appear to have a specific source. What's likely is that the plot is a response to folk tales, poems, and popular ballads of the day, such as the *The Merry Jest of a Shrewde and Curste Wyfe* (1553). The Bianca subplot comes from an English version of a 1509 Italian play, *I Suppositi*. But the general story line—a husband having to "tame" his unruly, disobedient wife—was a

Mr. John Drew as Petruchio, 1888

common theme in Shakespeare's day. The popularity of *The Taming of the Shrew* in its own time was great enough to inspire a famous sequel: John Fletcher's 1611 play *The Woman's Prize, or The Tamer Tamed*. In it, Petruchio remarries after Kate's death to someone who treats him the same as he had treated Kate.

Filmed eleven times, six as a silent movie, *The Taming of the Shrew* also inspired one of Broadway's most popular musicals, *Kiss Me, Kate*. Songwriter Cole Porter lent his great talent to an acclaimed score with titles such as "Brush Up Your Shakespeare," "I've

The suitors entreat Baptista for Bianca's hand on the streets of Padua.

Come to Wive It Wealthily in Padua," and "Always True to You (In My Fashion)." In the 1929 Mary Pickford/Douglas Fairbanks film, the lead characters take whips to each other. The 1966 Zeffirelli film starring real-life lovers Elizabeth Taylor as Kate and Richard Burton as Petruchio was even more boisterous, with Taylor attacking Burton with abandon (as well as crockery). In the 1990 New York Shakespeare Festival production, set in the American Old West, Morgan Freeman starred as Petruchio and Tracy Ullman as Kate, dressed like an Annie Oakley gunslinger. Her rambunctious portrayal included the usual "submission" speech but ended with Petruchio somehow laid out on the floor!

Clearly, Shakespeare's text and the choice of director allow very different readings of this play. Depending on tastes, *The Taming of the Shrew* can be seen as a feminist parable or a comic fantasy for male chauvinists. Or simply a delicious comic romp.

Timeline

1564	Shakespeare is baptized.
1568	Elizabeth I becomes Queen of England.
1572	Shakespeare begins grammar school.
1576	Opening of The Theatre, the first permanent playhouse in England.
1580	Drake sails around the world.
1582	Shakespeare marries Anne Hathaway.
1583	Shakespeare's daughter Susanna is baptized.
1585	Shakespeare's twins are baptized.
1588	Spanish Armada is defeated.
1592-94	Plague closes all of London's theaters.
1594	*Titus Andronicus* becomes first printed Shakespeare play.
1594	Shakespeare joins the Lord Chamberlain's Men.
1599	Lord Chamberlain's Men build the Globe Theatre; Shakespeare is part-owner of the building.
1609	Shakespeare's *Sonnets* published for the first time.
1610	Shakespeare retires to Stratford.
1613	Globe Theatre burns to the ground.
1616	William Shakespeare dies at the age of 52.
1623	Shakespeare's wife dies.
	First Folio published.

Reading
The Taming of the Shrew
Using This Parallel Text

This edition of *The Taming of the Shrew* is especially designed for readers who aren't familiar with Shakespeare. If you're fairly comfortable with his language, simply read the original text on the left-hand page. When you come to a confusing word or passage, refer to the modern English version on the right or the footnotes at the bottom.

If you think Elizabethan English doesn't even sound like English, read a passage of the modern version silently. Then read the same passage of the original. You'll find that Shakespeare's language begins to come alive for you. You may choose to work your way through the entire play this way.

As you read more, you'll probably find yourself using the modern version less and less. Remember, the parallel version is meant to be an aid, not a substitute for the original. If you read only the modern version, you'll cheat yourself out of Shakespeare's language—his quick-witted puns, sharp-tongued insults, and evocative images.

Keep in mind that language is a living thing, constantly growing and changing. New words are invented and new definitions for old words are added. Since Shakespeare wrote over four hundred years ago, it is not surprising that his work seems challenging to today's readers.

Here are some other reading strategies that can increase your enjoyment of the play.

Background

Knowing some historical background makes it easier to understand what's going on. You will find information about Shakespeare's life and Elizabethan theater at the back of this book. Reading the summaries that precede each act will also help you to follow the action of the play.

Getting the Beat

Like most dramatists of his time, Shakespeare frequently used **blank verse** in his plays. In blank verse, the text is written in measured lines that do not rhyme. Look at the following example from *The Taming of the Shrew*.

> Say that she rail, why then I'll tell her plain
> She sings as sweetly as a nightingale.
> Say that she frown, I'll say she looks as clear
> As morning roses newly wash'd with dew.

You can see that the four lines above are approximately equal in length, but they do not cover the whole width of the page as the lines in a story or essay might. They are, in fact, unrhymed verse with each line containing ten or eleven syllables. Furthermore, the ten syllables can be divided into five sections, called **iambs**, or feet. Each iamb contains one unstressed (**U**) and one stressed (**/**) syllable. Try reading the lines below, giving emphasis to the capitalized syllable in each iamb.

U /	U /	U /	U /	U /
Say THAT	she RAIL,	why THEN	I'll TELL	her PLAIN

U /	U /	U /	U /	U /
She SINGS	as SWEET	ly AS	a NIGHT	inGALE.

The length of a line of verse is measured by counting the stresses. This length is known as the **meter**. When there are five stresses and the rhythm follows an unstressed/stressed pattern, it is known as **iambic pentameter**. Much of Shakespeare's work is written in iambic pentameter.

Of course, Shakespeare was not rigid about this format. He sometimes varied the lines by putting accents in unusual places, by having lines with more or fewer than ten syllables, and by varying where pauses occur. An actor's interpretation can also add variety. (Only a terrible actor would deliver lines in a way that makes the rhythm sound singsong!)

Prose

In addition to verse, Shakespeare wrote speeches in **prose**, or language without rhythmic structure. Look at the dialogue in Act IV, Scene i, among Petruchio's servants. If you try beating out an iambic rhythm to these lines, you'll find it doesn't work because the characters are speaking in prose. Not until Petruchio arrives and scolds them ("You loggerheaded and unpolish'd grooms!") will you be able to find the rhythm of iambic pentameter again. Shakespeare often uses prose for comic speeches, to show madness, and for characters of lower social rank such as servants. His upper-class characters generally do not speak in prose. But these weren't hard and fast rules as far as Shakespeare was concerned. Whether characters speak in verse or prose is often a function of the situation and whom they're addressing, as well as their social status.

Contractions

As you know, contractions are words that have been combined by substituting an apostrophe for a letter or letters that have been removed. Contractions were as common in Shakespeare's time as they are today. For example, we use *it's* as a contraction for the words *it is*. In Shakespeare's writing you will discover that *'tis* means the same thing. Shakespeare often used the apostrophe to shorten words so that they would fit into the rhythmic pattern of a line. This is especially true of verbs ending in *-ed*. Note that in Shakespeare's plays, the *-ed* at the end of a verb is usually pronounced as a separate syllable. Therefore, *walked* would be pronounced as two syllables, *walk*ed*, while *walk'd* would be only one.

Speak and Listen

Remember that plays are written to be acted, not read silently. Reading aloud—whether in a group or alone—helps you to "hear" the meaning. Listening to another reader will also help. You might also enjoy listening to a recording of the play by professional actors.

Clues and Cues

Shakespeare was sparing in his use of stage directions. In fact, many of those in modern editions were added by later editors. Added stage directions are usually indicated by brackets. For example, [*aside*] tells the actor to give the audience information that the other characters can't hear.

Sometimes a character's actions are suggested by the lines themselves.

The Play's the Thing

Finally, if you can't figure out every word in the play, don't get discouraged. The people in Shakespeare's audience couldn't either. At that time, language was changing rapidly and standardized spelling, punctuation, grammar, and even dictionaries did not exist. Besides, Shakespeare loved to play with words. He made up new combinations, like *fat-guts* and *mumble-news*. To make matters worse, the actors probably spoke very rapidly. But the audience didn't strain to catch every word. They went to a Shakespeare play for the same reasons we go to a movie—to get caught up in the story and the acting, to have a great laugh or a good cry.

Cast of Characters

CHRISTOPHER SLY a beggar
HOSTESS of an alehouse
A LORD
HUNTSMEN of the Lord ⎫ characters in the Induction
PAGE (disguised as a lady)
PLAYERS
SERVINGMEN
MESSENGER

BAPTISTA MINOLA father to Katherine and Bianca
KATHERINE his elder daughter
BIANCA his younger daughter

PETRUCHIO suitor to Katherine

GREMIO
HORTENSIO (later disguised as the teacher Litio) ⎫ suitors to Bianca
LUCENTIO (later disguised as the teacher Cambio)

VINCENTIO, Lucentio's father

TRANIO (later impersonating Lucentio) ⎫ servants to Lucentio
BIONDELLO

A PEDANT (later disguised as Vincentio)

GRUMIO
CURTIS
NATHANIEL
PHILLIP ⎫ servants to Petruchio
JOSEPH
NICHOLAS
PETER

WIDOW

TAILOR
HABERDASHER
OFFICER
SERVANTS to Baptista and Petruchio

The Taming of
the Shrew

ACT 1

Elizabeth Taylor as Kate in a 1967 film directed by Franco Zeffirelli

*"Her only fault, and that is faults
enough, is that she is intolerable curst...."*

Before You Read

1. *The Taming of the Shrew* contains an introductory element called the Induction. As you read, think about why Shakespeare may have written these two introduction scenes.

2. Notice how Shakespeare's language helps to create a playful and comic atmosphere in Act I.

3. *The Taming of the Shrew* subsists of a main plot—the marriage and taming of the headstrong Kate—and a subplot, the wooing of her sister, Bianca. As you read, follow the strands of plot and subplot to see how they affect each other.

Literary Elements

1. An **allusion** is a reference to literary or historical sources outside the text that adds meaning to the story. In Act I, Scene i, Tranio's allusion to the rigorous philosopher Aristotle in the same breath with the Roman love poet Ovid is meant to remind his master, Lucentio, that his studies should not take priority over the pleasures of love.

2. **Foreshadowing** refers to hints about what might happen later in the play. In the Induction, a practical joke is played on the drunken tinker Christopher Sly. The Lord and his household pretend that Sly is a nobleman who has temporarily gone mad, and they "reintroduce" him to his good and beautiful wife. This trick foreshadows the rest of play being a bawdy comedy about reversals in fortunes and women who model the wifely virtues.

3. **Hyperbole** is exaggeration or overstatement not meant to be taken literally. As you might expect of a Shakespearean comedy, there are many examples of hyperbole in this play. For example, in Act I, Scene i, Gremio says he would as soon marry Kate as "be whipp'd at the high cross every morning."

Words to Know

The following vocabulary words appear in the Induction and Act I in the original text of Shakespeare's play. However, they are words that are still used today. Read the definitions here, and pay attention to the words as you read the play (they will be in boldfaced type).

Induction

abate	grow less; diminish
beguiled	deceived; hoodwinked
homage	honor; worship
incur	invite; open yourself up to
infused	mixed; combined
malady	difficulty; problem
procure	get; obtain
usurp	seize; take without permission

Act I

importune	beg; pester
ingrate	someone who is not thankful
largess	gift; generosity
perused [perus'd]	examined; looked over carefully
rhetoric	oratory; public speaking

Act Summary

A drunken beggar named Christopher Sly is tossed out of an alehouse by the landlady and found lying in the road by a local nobleman. For a practical joke, the Lord brings Sly home and directs his servants to pretend like the tinker is nobility.

When Sly wakes up in the Lord's manor, he is told of his amnesia and introduced to the lovely wife he supposedly forgot. He is excited to get to know her better, but their reunion must wait until a traveling group of actors has performed their play for him.

The play-within-the-play begins when Lucentio, a young nobleman, arrives in Padua with his servant, Tranio, for "a course of learning." In a public square, the two overhear a rich gentleman, Baptista, admonishing Hortensio and Gremio for courting his younger daughter, Bianca. Baptista will not allow Bianca to marry until her older sister, Kate, is wed, and since the latter is a legendary shrew, the two suitors think their prospects are dim.

They decide to help Baptista find a suitor for Kate.

Meanwhile, Lucentio thinks he has fallen in love with the fair Bianca. He decides to disguise himself as a scholar and get close to her by applying to become her language tutor. Meanwhile, Lucentio's servant, Tranio, will pretend to be Lucentio, the visiting young nobleman in town. He will try to persuade Baptista of his desirability as a husband to Bianca.

Petruchio arrives in Padua in search of a wife and learns from his friend Hortensio that the shrewish but rich Kate is available. Petruchio is confident that he can tame her and at once asks to meet Baptista to make arrangements.

Hortensio decides to go in disguise as a music tutor to Bianca. All three suitors to Bianca—Gremio, Hortensio, and Lucentio—will do all they can to help Petruchio woo Kate.

A modern interpretation of the Induction, Royal Shakespeare Theatre, 1992

INDUCTION, SCENE I

[*Before an alehouse on a heath.*] *Enter* HOSTESS *and beggar,* CHRISTOPHER SLY.

SLY

I'll feeze you, in faith.

HOSTESS

A pair of stocks, you rogue!

SLY

You're a baggage! The Slys are no rogues. Look in the chronicles; we came in with Richard Conqueror.*
5   Therefore, *paucas pallabris;** let the world slide. Sessa!

HOSTESS

You will not pay for the glasses you have burst?

SLY

No, not a denier. Go, by Jeronimy! Go to thy cold bed and warm thee.

HOSTESS

I know my remedy; I must go fetch the headborough.

[*Exit.*]

SLY

10   Third, or fourth, or fifth borough, I'll answer him by law.
I'll not budge an inch, boy; let him come, and kindly.

[*Falls asleep.*]

Wind horns. Enter a LORD *from hunting, with his* TRAIN.

LORD

Huntsman, I charge thee tender well my hounds.
Breathe Merriman, the poor cur is emboss'd;
And couple Clowder with the deep-mouth'd brach.
15   Saw'st thou not, boy, how Silver made it good
At the hedge corner, in the coldest fault?
I would not lose the dog for twenty pound!

---

4   *Richard*   Sly means William the Conqueror, whose Norman army invaded and conquered England in 1066.

5   *paucas pallabris* or *pocas palabras*   Spanish for "few words"

INDUCTION, SCENE 1

Outside a rural alehouse. HOSTESS *and beggar*
CHRISTOPHER SLY *enter.*

SLY

I'll get you, I will.

HOSTESS

I'll put you in the stocks, you rascal!

SLY

You wretch, the Slys aren't rascals. Look it up in the Chronicles:
we came to England with Richard the Conqueror. So, in short,
let the world go by. Shut up!   5

HOSTESS

You won't pay for the glasses you broke?

SLY

No, not a penny. Go, by Saint Jeronimy. Go to your cold bed
and warm yourself.

HOSTESS

I know what I have to do—I'd better get the constable.

> *Exits.*

SLY

Third, fourth, or fifth constable, I'll give him a lawful response.   10
I'll not budge an inch, wretch. Let him come, by all means.

> *Falls asleep.*

> *Horns blow. A* LORD *enters, returning from the hunt, with his*
> SERVANTS *and fellow* HUNTERS.

LORD

Huntsman, I order you to look after my hounds.
Let Merriman get his breath back—the poor dog is exhausted—
and mate Clowder with the deep-mouthed bitch.
Didn't you see, boy, how Silver proved his skill   15
at the corner of the hedge where the trail was coldest?
I wouldn't give up that dog for twenty pounds.

1. HUNTER

Why, Bellman is as good as he, my lord.
He cried upon it at the merest loss,
20   And twice today pick'd out the dullest scent.
Trust me, I take him for the better dog.

LORD

Thou art a fool. If Echo were as fleet,
I would esteem him worth a dozen such.
But sup them well and look unto them all;
25   Tomorrow I intend to hunt again.

1. HUNTER

I will, my lord.

LORD [*Points to* SLY.]

What's here? One dead, or drunk? See doth he breathe?

2. HUNTER

He breathes, my lord. Were he not warm'd with ale,
This were a bed but cold to sleep so soundly.

LORD

30   O monstrous beast, how like a swine he lies!
Grim death, how foul and loathsome is thine image!
Sirs, I will practise on this drunken man.
What think you, if he were convey'd to bed,
Wrapp'd in sweet clothes, rings put upon his fingers,
35   A most delicious banquet by his bed,
And brave attendants near him when he wakes,
Would not the beggar then forget himself?

1. HUNTER

Believe me, lord, I think he cannot choose.

2. HUNTER

It would seem strange unto him when he wak'd.

LORD

40   Even as a flatt'ring dream or worthless fancy.
Then take him up and manage well the jest.
Carry him gently to my fairest chamber,
And hang it round with all my wanton pictures.

FIRST HUNTSMAN

Why, Belman is just as good a dog as Silver, my lord.
He barked even when the trail was completely cold,
and twice today he sniffed out the faintest scent.   20
Believe me, I think he's the better dog.

LORD

You're a fool. If Echo were as fast,
I'd think he were worth a dozen like Silver.
But feed them well and look after them all.
I'm planning on hunting again tomorrow.   25

FIRST HUNTSMAN

I will, my lord.

LORD (*pointing to* SLY)

Who is this here? Is he dead or drunk? Check and see—is he
    still breathing?

SECOND HUNTSMAN

He's breathing, my lord. If he weren't warmed up with liquor,
he'd find this was a cold bed on which to sleep so soundly.

LORD

What a monstrous animal—he lies there just like a pig!   30
Grim death, your picture is foul and hateful!
Gentlemen, I'll play a trick on this drunk.
What would you think if we carried him to bed,
dressed him in fine clothes, put rings on his fingers,
set a delicious feast beside his bed,   35
and stationed well-dressed servants nearby when he
    awakened—
wouldn't the beggar forget who he was?

FIRST HUNTSMAN

Really, lord, I'd think he could hardly do anything else.

SECOND HUNTSMAN

Things would seem strange to him when he woke up.

LORD

As strange as an illusory dream or unreal fantasy.   40
Then pick him up, and let's carry out the joke in style.
Carry him gently to my best bedroom
and hang my liveliest pictures on the wall.

Balm his foul head in warm distilled waters,
45 And burn sweet wood to make the lodging sweet.
Procure me music ready when he wakes
To make a dulcet and a heavenly sound;
And if he chance to speak, be ready straight
And, with a low submissive reverence,
50 Say "What is it your Honour will command?"
Let one attend him with a silver basin
Full of rosewater and bestrew'd with flowers,
Another bear the ewer, the third a diaper,
And say, "Will 't please your Lordship cool your hands?"
55 Someone be ready with a costly suit,
And ask him what apparel he will wear.
Another tell him of his hounds and horse,
And that his lady mourns at his disease.
Persuade him that he hath been lunatic,
60 And when he says he is, say that he dreams,
For he is nothing but a mighty lord.
This do and do it kindly, gentle sirs.
It will be pastime passing excellent,
If it be husbanded with modesty.

3. HUNTER
65 My lord, I warrant you we will play our part
As he shall think by our true diligence
He is no less than what we say he is.

LORD
Take him up gently and to bed with him;
And each one to his office when he wakes.

[*Some bear out* SLY.] *Sound trumpets.*

70 Sirrah,* go see what trumpet 'tis that sounds.

[*Exit* SERVINGMAN.]

Belike some noble gentleman that means
Traveling some journey to repose him here.

Enter SERVINGMAN.

How now! Who is it?

---

70 *Sirrah*   a term used to address someone of lower status than the speaker. The
word was also used as a snub.

Wash his dirty head in warm, scented water,
and burn sweet-smelling wood to perfume the room. 45
Get some musicians ready so when he awakens,
they can play a sweet and heavenly tune.
And if he should speak, be ready immediately
and with a humble, submissive, reverent tone
say, "What does your Honor desire?" 50
Let someone present him with a silver bowl
full of rose water, sprinkled with flowers;
another carry the pitcher; a third one carry a towel
and say, "Does your Lordship wish to cool your hands?"
Someone bring in an expensive suit 55
and ask him what clothes he wants to wear.
Someone else tell him about his dogs and horses
and that his wife is heartbroken about his disorder.
Convince him that he has been a lunatic,
and when he says he must be one now, tell him he's dreaming 60
because he's nothing else except a mighty lord.
Do all this, and make it convincing, gentlemen.
It will be wonderful entertainment
if carried out with a straight face.

THIRD HUNTSMAN

My lord, I guarantee you we'll play our parts 65
so he'll think, from our earnest attentions,
that he is nothing less than what we say he is.

LORD

Pick him up gently and carry him to bed,
and everyone take their places when he awakens.

Sly is carried out. Trumpets are blown.

Servant, go and see who is blowing that trumpet. 70

SERVANT exits.

It's probably a nobleman on a trip
who intends to rest here.

SERVANT enters.

Well, then, who is it?

SERVANT

An 't please your Honour, players
75 That offer service to your Lordship.

LORD

Bid them come near. [*Enter* PLAYERS.]
Now, fellows, you are welcome.

PLAYERS

We thank your Honour.

LORD

Do you intend to stay with me tonight?

1. PLAYER

So please your Lordship to accept our duty.

LORD

80 With all my heart. This fellow I remember
Since once he play'd a farmer's eldest son.—
'Twas where you woo'd the gentlewoman so well.
I have forgot your name, but sure that part
Was aptly fitted and naturally performed.

2. PLAYER

85 I think 'twas Soto* that your Honour means.

LORD

'Tis very true. Thou didst it excellent.
Well, you are come to me in happy time,
The rather for I have some sport in hand
Wherein your cunning can assist me much.
90 There is a lord will hear you play tonight;
But I am doubtful of your modesties,
Lest, over-eyeing of his odd behaviour—
For yet his Honour never heard a play—
You break into some merry passion
95 And so offend him; for I tell you, sirs,
If you should smile he grows impatient.

1. PLAYER

Fear not, my lord, we can contain ourselves
Were he the veriest antic in the world.

---

85   *Soto*   a character who appears in John Fletcher's play *Women Pleased*

SERVANT

If it please your Honor, it is a troupe of actors
who offer to perform for you.   75

LORD

Tell them to come here. (PLAYERS *enter.*) Well, gentlemen,
welcome.

PLAYERS

Thank you, your Honor.

LORD

Do you intend to stay here tonight?

FIRST PLAYER

If your Lordship will accept our services.

LORD

Gladly, I remember this fellow   80
from the time he played a farmer's eldest son—
when you courted the lady so well.
I've forgotten your name, but really, that part
suited you well, and you performed it naturally.

SECOND PLAYER

I think it was the part of Soto your Honor remembers.   85

LORD

That's right. You acted it very well.
Well, you've arrived at just the right moment,
especially because I have something amusing cooking,
in which your talents will really help me.
There is a lord who will watch your play tonight.   90
But I'm skeptical about your ability to keep a straight face
for fear that seeing his odd behavior—
because this lord has never seen a play before—
you might break into a fit of laughter
and then offend him. I tell you, gentlemen,   95
if you should as much as smile, he will be irked.

FIRST PLAYER

Don't worry, my lord, we can control our laughter,
even if he's the worst eccentric in the world.

LORD [*to a* SERVINGMAN]

Go, sirrah, take them to the buttery

100 And give them friendly welcome every one.

Let them want nothing that my house affords.

One exits with the PLAYERS.

Sirrah, go you to Barthol'mew, my page,

And see him dress'd in all suits like a lady.

That done, conduct him to the drunkard's chamber,

105 And call him "Madam," do him obeisance.

Tell him from me, as he will win my love,

He bear himself with honourable action,

Such as he hath observ'd in noble ladies

Unto their lords, by them accomplished.

110 Such duty to the drunkard let him do

With soft low tongue and lowly courtesy,

And say, "What is 't your Honour will command,

Wherein your lady and your humble wife

May show her duty and make known her love?"

115 And then with kind embracements, tempting kisses,

And with declining head into his bosom,

Bid him shed tears, as being overjoy'd

To see her noble lord restor'd to health,

Who for this seven years hath esteemed him

120 No better than a poor and loathsome beggar.

And if the boy have not a woman's gift

To rain a shower of commanded tears,

An onion will do well for such a shift,

Which (in a napkin being close convey'd)

125 Shall in despite enforce a watery eye.

See this dispatch'd with all the haste thou canst;

Anon I'll give thee more instructions.

A SERVINGMAN *exits.*

I know the boy will well **usurp** the grace,

Voice, gait, and action of a gentlewoman.

130 I long to hear him call the drunkard "husband"!

And how my men will stay themselves from laughter

LORD

Go, servant, take them to the pantry,
and give them all a friendly welcome.   100
Get them anything in the house they want.

      SERVANT *and* PLAYERS *exit.*

Servant, go to Bartholomew, my page,
and see that he dresses just like a lady.
When that's done, lead him to the drunk's bedroom,
and call him "Madam," and give him respect.   105
Tell him that I said—if he wants to win my love—
that he should act honorably,
just as he's seen noble ladies
act toward their husbands.
Tell my page to greet the drunkard respectfully,   110
with a soft, modest voice and humble courtesy,
and say, "What do you command, your Honor,
that your lady and humble wife can do for you
to show her duty and make known her love?"
And then, with kind embraces, tempting kisses,   115
and with his head bowed to his breast,
tell him to shed tears, as if "she" were overjoyed
to see "her" noble lord well again
after he had for seven years believed himself to be
no better than a poor, disgusting beggar.   120
And if the boy doesn't have the woman's knack
for crying up a storm whenever he wants,
an onion will do the trick—
which, if it's secretly carried in a handkerchief,
can't fail to bring tears to the eyes.   125
See that these preparations are made as quickly as possible.
I'll give you more instructions soon.

      SERVANT *exits.*

I know the boy will skillfully mimic the grace,
voice, walk, and actions of a lady.
I can't wait to hear him call the drunk "husband."   130
How will my servants keep from laughing

When they do **homage** to this simple peasant.
I'll in to counsel them; haply my presence
May well **abate** the over-merry spleen
135   Which otherwise would grow into extremes.

　　　[*Exeunt.*]

when they pretend to serve this simple peasant?
I'll go and give them some advice. Maybe my presence
can stifle their overly merry spirit,
which otherwise might get out of hand.   135

    They exit.

INDUCTION, SCENE II

[A bedchamber in the Lord's house.] Enter aloft the drunkard SLY, richly dressed, with ATTENDANTS: some with apparel, basin and ewer, and other appurtenances; and LORD, like a servant.

SLY
For God's sake, a pot of small ale.

1. SERVANT
Will 't please your Lord drink a cup of sack?

2. SERVANT
Will 't please your Honour taste of these conserves?

3. SERVANT
What raiment will your Honour wear today?

SLY
5   I am Christophero Sly! Call not me "Honour" nor "Lordship." I ne'er drank sack in my life. An if you give me any conserves, give me conserves of beef. Ne'er ask me what raiment I'll wear, for I have no more doublets than backs, no more stockings than legs, nor no more shoes
10   than feet, nay sometime more feet than shoes, or such shoes as my toes look through the over-leather.

LORD [*as* ATTENDANT]
Heaven cease this idle humour in your Honour!
O, that a mighty man of such descent,
Of such possessions, and so high esteem,
15   Should be **infused** with so foul a spirit!

SLY
What, would you make me mad? Am not I Christopher Sly, old Sly's son of Burton Heath, by birth a pedlar, by education a cardmaker,* by transmutation a bearherd, and now by present profession a tinker? Ask Marian
20   Hacket, the fat alewife of Wincot, if she know me not. If she say I am not fourteen pence on the score for sheer ale, score me up for the lying'st knave in Christendom. What! I am not bestraught! Here's—

---

18   *cardmaker*   Sly means cards used to separate wool before it was spun.

INDUCTION, SCENE 2

Bedroom in the Lord's house. SLY, ATTENDANTS (*carrying clothing, bowl, pitcher, and other items*) *and the* LORD, *dressed like a servant.*

SLY
For God's sake, give me a pot of cheap ale!

FIRST SERVANT
Would your Worship like a cup of sherry to drink?

SECOND SERVANT
Would your honor like a taste of the fruit conserves?

THIRD SERVANT
What clothes will your Honor wear today?

SLY
I'm Christopher Sly. Don't call me your Honor or your Lordship,   5
I never drank sherry in my life, and if you give me any conserves,
make it salt beef. Never ask me what clothes I want to wear
since I don't have any more doublets than I have backs, no
more stockings than I have legs, and no more shoes than I
have feet—no, sometimes more feet than shoes, or such   10
shoes as my toes can see through.

LORD, *as* ATTENDANT
Heaven cure your Honor's mad fantasy!
It's terrible that a mighty man of such noble ancestors,
such belongings, and such good reputation
should be possessed by such a foul spirit!   15

SLY
Are you trying to drive me crazy? Aren't I Christopher Sly, old
Sly's son from Barton-on-the-Heath? Born a peddler, trained
to be a cardmaker, changed to a bear trainer, and now working
as a tinker? Ask Marian Hacket, the fat tavernkeeper at Wincot,   20
if she doesn't know me. If she says I don't have fourteen pence
on my tab for ale alone, chalk me up as the biggest liar in the
Christian world. Indeed, I'm not crazy! Here's—

3. SERVANT

    O, this it is that makes your lady mourn!

2. SERVANT

25   O, this is it that makes your servants droop!

LORD [*as* ATTENDANT]

    Hence comes it that your kindred shuns your house,
    As beaten hence by your strange lunacy.
    O noble lord, bethink thee of thy birth,
    Call home thy ancient thoughts from banishment
30   And banish hence these abject lowly dreams.
    Look how thy servants do attend on thee,
    Each in his office ready at thy beck.
    Wilt thou have music? Hark! Apollo* plays,

        [*music*]

    And twenty caged nightingales do sing.
35   Or wilt thou sleep? We'll have thee to a couch
    Softer and sweeter than the lustful bed
    On purpose trimm'd up for Semiramis.*
    Say thou wilt walk; we will bestrew the ground.
    Or wilt thou ride? Thy horses shall be trapp'd,
40   Their harness studded all with gold and pearl.
    Dost thou love hawking*? Thou hast hawks will soar
    Above the morning lark. Or wilt thou hunt?
    Thy hounds shall make the welkin answer them
    And fetch shrill echoes from the hollow earth.

1. SERVANT

45   Say thou wilt course; thy greyhounds are as swift
    As breathed stags, ay, fleeter than the roe.

2. SERVANT

    Dost thou love pictures? We will fetch thee straight
    Adonis* painted by a running brook,

---

33 *Apollo* Greek sun god and god of music

37 *Semiramis* legendary queen of Assyria, renowned for her lustful nature and great beauty

41 *hawking* using trained birds to hunt

48 *Adonis* one of Aphrodite's (or Cytherea's) lovers. Aphrodite was the Greek goddess of love.

THIRD SERVANT
This is the kind of thing that breaks your wife's heart!

SECOND SERVANT
This is the kind of thing that makes your servants despair!   25

LORD, *as* ATTENDANT
This is the reason that your relatives avoid your house,
chased away from here by your strange madness.
Oh noble lord, think about your noble standing.
Call back your old, sane thoughts from exile,
and banish your pathetic, beggarly dreams.   30
Look at how your servants wait on you,
everyone in his place, ready to do as you command.
Do you want music? Listen, Apollo is playing,

> *Music plays.*

and twenty caged nightingales are singing.
Or do you want to sleep? We'll take you to a bed   35
softer and nicer than the lustful bed
prepared for Semiramis.
If you say you want to walk, we'll scatter the ground with
   rushes and flowers.
Or do you want to ride? Your horses will be decorated,
their harness studded all over with gold and pearls.   40
Do you love hawking? You have hawks that will soar
above the morning lark. Or do you want to hunt?
Your hounds will make the sky answer their barks
and produce shrill echoes from the hollow earth.

FIRST SERVANT
Say that you want to hunt hares; your greyhounds are as swift   45
as strong stags and faster than small deer.

SECOND SERVANT
Do you love pictures? We'll bring you at once
Adonis, pictured by a running brook

And Cytherea all in sedges hid,
50 Which seem to move and wanton with her breath,
Even as the waving sedges play with wind.

LORD [*as* ATTENDANT]
We'll show thee Io* as she was a maid,
And how she was **beguiled** and surprised,
As lively painted as the deed was done.

3. SERVANT
55 Or Daphne* roaming through a thorny wood,
Scratching her legs that one shall swear she bleeds,
And at that sight shall sad Apollo weep,
So workmanly the blood and tears are drawn.

LORD [*as* ATTENDANT]
Thou art a lord and nothing but a lord.
60 Thou hast a lady far more beautiful
Than any woman in this waning age.

1. SERVANT
And till the tears that she hath shed for thee
Like envious floods o'errun her lovely face,
She was the fairest creature in the world—
65 And yet she is inferior to none.

SLY
Am I a lord? And have I such a lady?
Or do I dream? Or have I dream'd till now?
I do not sleep: I see, I hear, I speak,
I smell sweet savours, and I feel soft things.
70 Upon my life, I am a lord indeed
And not a tinker, nor Christopher Sly.
Well, bring our lady hither to our sight,
And once again a pot o' th' smallest ale.

2. SERVANT
Will 't please your Mightiness to wash your hands?
75 O, how we joy to see your wit restor'd!
O, that once more you knew but what you are!

---

52   *Io*   a Greek girl loved by Zeus, the king of the gods

55   *Daphne*   a nymph who was chased by the amorous Apollo. Her father saved her by changing her into a tree.

and Cytherea, hidden in the marsh grasses,
which seem to move and sway with her breath,   50
just like the waving marsh grasses dance in the wind.

LORD, *as* ATTENDANT
We'll show you a picture of Io, showing her as a girl,
and how she was seduced and tricked.
It's so lifelike, it's like seeing it really happen.

THIRD SERVANT
Or Daphne, wandering through a thorny wood,   55
scratching her legs so that the viewer would swear she bleeds.
And sad Apollo will weep at the sight,
the blood and tears are drawn so skillfully!

LORD, *as* ATTENDANT
You are a lord, pure and simple,
and you have a wife far more beautiful   60
than any other woman in these declining days.

FIRST SERVANT
And before the tears that she cried for you
overran her lovely face like envious floods,
she was the most beautiful woman in the world.
Even now, no one is more lovely than she is.   65

SLY
Am I a lord, and am I married to such a woman?
Or am I dreaming? Or have I been dreaming until now?
I'm not sleeping now—I see, hear, speak,
smell sweet smells, and feel soft things.
I declare, I really am a lord   70
and not a tinker or Christopher Sly.
Well, bring my wife here to me,
and I ask you once again, bring a pot of the weakest ale.

SECOND SERVANT
Would you like to wash your hands, your Honor?
Oh how happy we are to see you sane again!   75
How long we've wished that once again you would realize
    who you are!

These fifteen years you have been in a dream,
Or, when you wak'd, so wak'd as if you slept.

SLY

These fifteen years! By my fay, a goodly nap.
80   But did I never speak of all that time?

1. SERVANT

O, yes, my lord, but very idle words.
For though you lay here in this goodly chamber,
Yet would you say ye were beaten out of door,
And rail upon the hostess of the house,
85   And say you would present her at the leet
Because she brought stone jugs and no seal'd quarts.
Sometimes you would call out for Cicely Hacket.

SLY

Ay, the woman's maid of the house.

3. SERVANT

Why, sir, you know no house nor no such maid,
90   Nor no such men as you have reckon'd up,
As Stephen Sly and old John Naps of Greete,
And Peter Turph and Henry Pimpernell,*
And twenty more such names and men as these
Which never were, nor no man ever saw.

SLY

95   Now, Lord be thanked for my good amends!

ALL

Amen.

Enter the PAGE as a lady, with ATTENDANTS.

SLY

I thank thee. Thou shalt not lose by it.

PAGE [as LADY]

How fares my noble lord?

91–92   *Stephen Sly, etc.*   Stephen Sly was a real resident of Stratford,
Shakespeare's birthplace. All the others named here may be real people. Greete
may be a misprint for Green, a town near Stratford.

For the past fifteen years, you've been dreaming,
or when you were awake, it was like you were still asleep.

SLY
The past fifteen years! My word, that's a good nap!
But didn't I ever say anything during all that time? 80

FIRST SERVANT
Oh yes, my lord, but they were meaningless words,
for even while you were lying here in this fine bedroom,
you'd say you'd been chased out the door.
And you'd complain about the hostess of the tavern
and say you'd accuse her at the court before the manor lord 85
because she served her liquor in stone jugs and not in clearly
    marked quart jars.
Sometimes you would call out for Cicely Hacket.

SLY
Yes, that was the lady's maid at the tavern.

THIRD SERVANT
Why, sir, you don't know of any such tavern or maid.
Or any of the men you talked about such 90
as Stephen Sly, old John Naps of Greete,
Peter Turph, and Henry Pimpernell,
and twenty more names and men such as these
who never really existed and whom no one ever saw.

SLY
Well, thank God for my excellent recovery! 95

ALL
Amen.

    The PAGE *enters, dressed as a woman, with* ATTENDANTS.

SLY
Thank you. You'll be rewarded for your good wishes.

PAGE, *as* LADY
How are you, my noble lord?

SLY

    Marry, I fare well, for here is cheer enough.
100   Where is my wife?

PAGE [*as* LADY]

    Here, noble lord. What is thy will with her?

SLY

    Are you my wife, and will not call me "husband"?
    My men should call me "lord"; I am your goodman.

PAGE [*as* LADY]

    My husband and my lord, my lord and husband,
105   I am your wife in all obedience.

SLY

    I know it well.—What must I call her?

LORD [*as* ATTENDANT]

    "Madam."

SLY

    "Alice Madam" or "Joan Madam"?*

LORD [*as* ATTENDANT]

    "Madam," and nothing else. So lords call ladies.

SLY

110   Madam wife, they say that I have dream'd
    And slept above some fifteen year or more.

PAGE [*as* LADY]

    Ay, and the time seems thirty unto me,
    Being all this time abandon'd from your bed.

SLY

    'Tis much.—Servants, leave me and her alone.—
115   Madam, undress you, and come now to bed.

PAGE [*as* LADY]

    Thrice noble lord, let me entreat of you
    To pardon me yet for a night or two,
    Or if not so, until the sun be set;
    For your physicians have expressly charg'd,

---

108   *Alice . . . Joan* Sly gives his "lady" humorously common names.

SLY

Indeed, I'm doing quite well, for this is a pleasing situation.
Where is my wife?   100

PAGE, *as* LADY

I am your wife, noble lord. What can I do for you?

SLY

You're my wife, and yet you don't call me "husband"?
My servants should call me "lord." You should call me "husband".

PAGE, *as* LADY

You are my husband and my lord, my lord and husband.
I am your obedient wife.   105

SLY

I'm certain of that. What should I call her?

LORD, *as* ATTENDANT

"Madam".

SLY

"Alice Madam," or "Joan Madam"?

LORD, *as* ATTENDANT

Just "madam." That's what lords call their ladies.

SLY

Madam wife, they say I've dreamed   110
and slept for fifteen years or more.

PAGE, *as* LADY

Yes, and it seems like thirty years to me
since I've been a stranger to your bed all this time.

SLY

That is a long time. Servants, leave me and my wife alone.

SERVANTS *exit.*

Madam, undress and come to bed.   115

PAGE, *as* LADY

My most noble lord, I beg you
to excuse me from coming to bed with you for a night or two.
Or if not for that long, at least until sunset.
Your doctors have strictly ordered

120 In peril to **incur** your former **malady**,
That I should yet absent me from your bed.
I hope this reason stands for my excuse.

SLY

Ay, it stands so that I may hardly tarry so long, but I
would be loath to fall into my dreams again. I will
125 therefore tarry in despite of the flesh and the blood.

Enter a MESSENGER.

MESSENGER

Your Honour's players, hearing your amendment,
Are come to play a pleasant comedy,
For so your doctors hold it very meet,
Seeing too much sadness* hath congeal'd your blood,
130 And melancholy is the nurse of frenzy.
Therefore they thought it good you hear a play
And frame your mind to mirth and merriment,
Which bars a thousand harms and lengthens life.

SLY

Marry,* I will. Let them play it. [MESSENGER *exits.*] Is not
135 a comonty* a Christmas gambold or a tumbling trick?

PAGE [*as* LADY]

No, my good lord, it is more pleasing stuff.

SLY

What, household stuff?

PAGE [*as* LADY]

It is a kind of history.

SLY

Well, we'll see 't. Come, madam wife, sit by my side, and
140 let the world slip. We shall ne'er be younger.

[*They all sit.*] *Flourish.*

---

129   *sadness* Elizabethans believed that sorrow affected the blood in this way.

134   *marry* originally from the oath "by the Virgin Mary." By Shakespeare's day, it
had become an intensifier like "really" or "indeed."

135   *comonty* Sly's pronunciation of comedy

that, to avoid the risk of further madness,   120
I should not sleep with you, yet.
I hope this explanation will stand as my excuse.

SLY

Yes, it stands so that I can hardly wait another minute; but I
would hate to fall back into my delusions. Therefore, I'll wait,
despite the urges of my flesh and blood.   125

A MESSENGER *enters.*

MESSENGER

Your Honor's acting troupe, hearing that you were better,
have come to perform a pleasant comedy.
Your doctors think it would be very good for you,
since your blood has been congealed by too much sadness,
and melancholy is the germ of insanity.   130
Therefore, they thought it would be a good idea if you
    watched a play
and switched to thinking about comedy and humor,
which will prevent a thousand harmful things and lengthen
    your life.

SLY

Indeed, I'll let them act their play. Isn't a comonty a Christmas
game or an acrobatic trick?   135

PAGE, *as* LADY

No, my good lord. It's more amusing than that.

SLY

What! Is it household stuff, then?

PAGE, *as* LADY

It's a kind of story.

SLY

Well, I'll watch it. Come, my wife, and sit by my side, and let the
    world pass by. We'll never be any younger.   140

They sit and watch. Trumpet fanfare.

ACT I, SCENE I

[Padua. A public place.] Enter LUCENTIO *and his man*
TRANIO.

LUCENTIO

Tranio, since for the great desire I had
To see fair Padua, nursery of arts,
I am arriv'd for fruitful Lombardy,
The pleasant garden of great Italy,
5   And by my father's love and leave am arm'd
With his good will and thy good company.
My trusty servant, well approv'd in all,
Here let us breathe and haply institute
A course of learning and ingenious studies.
10 Pisa, renowned for grave citizens,
Gave me my being and my father first,
A merchant of great traffic through the world,
Vincentio, come of the Bentivolii.
Vincentio's son, brought up in Florence,
15 It shall become to serve all hopes conceiv'd
To deck his fortune with his virtuous deeds;
And therefore, Tranio, for the time I study
Virtue, and that part of philosophy
Will I apply that treats of happiness
20 By virtue specially to be achiev'd.
Tell me thy mind; for I have Pisa left
And am to Padua come, as he that leaves
A shallow plash to plunge him in the deep
And with satiety seeks to quench his thirst.

TRANIO

25 *Mi perdonato,* gentle master mine.
I am in all affected as yourself,
Glad that you thus continue your resolve
To suck the sweets of sweet philosophy.
Only, good master, while we do admire
30 This virtue and this moral discipline,
Let's be no stoics nor no stocks, I pray,
Or so devote to Aristotle's checks

ACT 1, SCENE 1

Padua, a public place. LUCENTIO *and his servant* TRANIO *enter.*

LUCENTIO
Tranio, since I really wanted
to see beautiful Padua, known as a cultural center,
I've come to rich Lombardy,
great Italy's pleasant garden spot.
And since, with my father's love and his permission, I've been
given   5
his approval and your good company—
you, my trusty, reliable servant—
let's stay here awhile and perhaps begin
a course of learning and challenging studies.
Pisa, famous for dignified citizens,   10
was my birthplace and before that, the birthplace of my father—
a merchant with a large trading market throughout the world—
Vincentio, a descendant of the Bentivolii.
Being Vincentio's son, raised in Florence,
it's fitting that I should do everything hoped of me   15
and make my fortune by good deeds.
Therefore, Tranio, I intend to study
virtue and similar knowledge
that relates to the kind of happiness
that can be found especially through goodness.   20
Tell me what you're thinking, for I've left Pisa
and come to Padua like a man who leaves
a shallow pool to plunge into deep waters
and quench his thirst to the fullest.

TRANIO
Pardon me, my gentle master,   25
I feel as you do about everything.
I'm glad that you're sticking to your decision
to study the joys of sweet philosophy.
Only, good master, while we're admiring
this virtue and this moral discipline,   30
let's not be stoics or unfeeling sticks, please,
or be so devoted to Aristotle's restrictions

As Ovid* be an outcast quite abjur'd.
Balk logic with acquaintance that you have,
35 And practise **rhetoric** in your common talk.
Music and poesy use to quicken you;
The mathematics and the metaphysics—
Fall to them as you find your stomach serves you.
No profit grows where is no pleasure ta'en.
40 In brief, sir, study what you most affect.

LUCENTIO
Gramercies, Tranio, well dost thou advise.
If, Biondello, thou wert come ashore,
We could at once put us in readiness
And take a lodging fit to entertain
45 Such friends as time in Padua shall beget.

> *Enter* BAPTISTA, KATHERINE, BIANCA, GREMIO, *a*
> *pantaloon,* * and HORTENSIO. LUCENTIO *and*
> TRANIO *stand by.*

But stay awhile, what company is this?

TRANIO
Master, some show to welcome us to town.

BAPTISTA [*to* GREMIO *and* HORTENSIO]
Gentlemen, **importune** me no farther,
For how I firmly am resolv'd you know:
50 That is, not to bestow my youngest daughter
Before I have a husband for the elder.
If either of you both love Katherine,
Because I know you well and love you well,
Leave shall you have to court her at your pleasure.

GREMIO
55 To cart her,* rather; she's too rough for me.—
There, there, Hortensio, will you any wife?

---

33 *Ovid* a Roman famous for his love poetry. He was banished by Emperor
Augustus.

s.d. *pantaloon* a comic old miser

55 *cart her* Both prostitutes and shrewish women were sometimes punished by
being exhibited to the public on carts.

that we completely reject the outcast Ovid.
Try out your logic with friends,
and practice rhetoric in your everyday conversation. 35
Use music and poetry to stimulate you.
Explore mathematics and metaphysics
as it suits you.
There's no profit where there isn't some pleasure.
So, in short, sir, study what you like best. 40

LUCENTIO
Thanks very much, Tranio. You've advised me well.
If only Biondello had come ashore,
we could get ready at once
and find a place to stay that's fit to entertain
such friends as, in time, I'll make in Padua. 45

> BAPTISTA; *his two daughters* KATHERINE *and* BIANCA;
> GREMIO, *a pantaloon; and* HORTENSIO, *Bianca's suitor, all*
> *enter.* LUCENTIO *and* TRANIO *stand nearby.*

But wait a minute—who are these people?

TRANIO
Some kind of show to welcome us to town, master.

BAPTISTA [*to* GREMIO *and* HORTENSIO]
Gentlemen, don't plead with me anymore.
Just how determined I am, you know.
I won't give away my youngest daughter 50
before my elder daughter has a husband.
If either one of you loves Katherine,
and since I know and love both of you well,
I'll give you permission to court her whenever you want.

GREMIO
To parade her around in a cart, you mean—she's too rough
for me. 55
How about you, Hortensio—how would you like to marry her?

KATHERINE [*to* BAPTISTA]
 I pray you, sir, is it your will
 To make a stale* of me amongst these mates?*

HORTENSIO
 "Mates," maid? How mean you that? No mates for you,
60 Unless you were of gentler, milder mould.

KATHERINE
 I' faith, sir, you shall never need to fear.
 Iwis it is not halfway to her heart;
 But if it were, doubt not her care should be
 To comb your noddle with a three-legg'd stool
65 And paint your face and use you like a fool.

HORTENSIO
 From all such devils, good Lord, deliver us!

GREMIO
 And me too, good Lord!

TRANIO [*aside to* LUCENTIO]
 Hush, master! Here's some good pastime toward.
 That wench is stark mad or wonderful froward.

LUCENTIO [*aside to* TRANIO]
70 But in the other's silence do I see
 Maid's mild behaviour and sobriety.
 Peace, Tranio!

TRANIO [*aside to* LUCENTIO]
 Well said, master. Mum, and gaze your fill.

BAPTISTA [*to* GREMIO *and* HORTENSIO]
 Gentlemen, that I may soon make good
75 What I have said— Bianca, get you in;
 And let it not displease thee, good Bianca,
 For I will love thee ne'er the less, my girl.

KATHERINE
 A pretty peat! It is best
 Put finger in the eye, and she knew why.

---

58 *stale* means both "laughingstock" and "prostitute." Katherine is also playing on the word "mate" ("stalemate").

58 *mates* means "brutes," "fellows," and "husbands"

KATHERINE (*to* BAPTISTA)

I ask you, sir, do you want
to make a fool of me among these brutish suitors?

HORTENSIO

"Suitors," girl! What do you mean by that? Not your suitors
unless you had a gentler, milder temperament. 60

KATHERINE

Truly, sir, you have nothing to fear.
Certainly I'm not even interested in marriage.
But if I were interested, don't doubt that I'd
comb your noodle with a stool
and bloody your face and treat you like a fool. 65

HORTENSIO

From all devils like her, deliver us, good Lord!

GREMIO

And me, too, good Lord!

TRANIO

Listen, master! Here's something entertaining brewing.
That woman is stark mad or amazingly willful.

LUCENTIO

But in the other girl's silence I see 70
ladylike gentle behavior and dignity.
Quiet, Tranio!

TRANIO

Well put, master. I'll be quiet, and you look all you want.

BAPTISTA (*to* GREMIO *and* HORTENSIO)

Gentlemen, I'll immediately do as
I told you I would—Bianca, go inside. 75
And don't be unhappy, my good Bianca,
because I love you as always, my girl.

KATHERINE

A fine pet! She should
be crying if she had any sense.

BIANCA

80   Sister, content you in my discontent.—
    Sir, to your pleasure humbly I subscribe.
    My books and instruments shall be my company,
    On them to look and practise by myself.

LUCENTIO [*aside to* TRANIO]

    Hark, Tranio! Thou may'st hear Minerva* speak!

HORTENSIO

85   Signior Baptista, will you be so strange?
    Sorry am I that our goodwill effects
    Bianca's grief.

GREMIO

                  Why will you mew her up,
    Signior Baptista, for this fiend of hell,
90   And make her bear the penance of her tongue?

BAPTISTA

    Gentlemen, content ye; I am resolv'd.—
    Go in, Bianca.

       [*Exit* BIANCA.]

    And for I know she taketh most delight
    In music, instruments, and poetry,
95   Schoolmasters will I keep within my house
    Fit to instruct her youth. If you, Hortensio,
    Or, Signior Gremio, you know any such,
    Prefer them hither; for to cunning men
    I will be very kind, and liberal
100   To mine own children in good bringing up.
    And so, farewell.—Katherine, you may stay,
    For I have more to commune with Bianca.

       [*Exit.*]

KATHERINE

    Why, and I trust I may go too, may I not?
    What, shall I be appointed hours, as though, belike,
105   I knew not what to take and what to leave? Ha!

       [*Exit.*]

---

84   *Minerva* Greek goddess of wisdom

BIANCA

Sister, be content with my unhappiness. 80
Sir, I'll humbly obey your wishes.
My books and instruments will be my company,
and I'll devote myself to them and practice.

LUCENTIO

Listen, Tranio—you can hear Minerva speaking.

HORTENSIO

Signor Baptista, will you be so unkind? 85
I'm sorry that our goodwill has been the cause of
Bianca's sorrow.

GREMIO

Will you cage her up,
Signor Baptista, on account of this devil,
and punish Bianca for her sister's shrewishness? 90

BAPTISTA

Gentlemen, be content. My decision is final.
Go inside, Bianca.

    BIANCA exits.

Since I know she is most delighted by
music, instruments, and poetry,
I'll board teachers in my house 95
who can properly instruct her. If you, Hortensio,
or you, Signor Gremio, know of any such teachers,
recommend that they come here. I'll be very kind
to clever men—and generous
to my own children in educating them. 100
And so, goodbye. Katherine, you must wait here
because I have something more to say to Bianca.

    BAPTISTA exits.

KATHERINE

Why, I trust I can leave, too, can't I?
Really, shall I be given a schedule as though
I didn't know when to stay and when to leave? Ha! 105

    KATHERINE exits.

GREMIO

You may go to the devil's dam. Your gifts are so good,
here's none will hold you.—Their love is not so great,
Hortensio, but we may blow our nails together and fast it
fairly out. Our cake's dough on both sides. Farewell. Yet,
110   for the love I bear my sweet Bianca, if I can by any means
light on a fit man to teach her that wherein she delights, I
will wish him to her father.

HORTENSIO

So will I, Signior Gremio. But a word, I pray. Though the
nature of our quarrel yet never brook'd parle, know now
115   upon advice, it toucheth us both, that we may yet again
have access to our fair mistress and be happy rivals in
Bianca's love, to labour and effect one thing specially.

GREMIO

What's that, I pray?

HORTENSIO

Marry, sir, to get a husband for her sister.

GREMIO

120   A husband! A devil!

HORTENSIO

I say "a husband."

GREMIO

I say "a devil." Think'st thou, Hortensio, though her father
be very rich, any man is so very a fool to be married to hell?

HORTENSIO

Tush, Gremio. Though it pass your patience and mine to
125   endure her loud alarums, why, man, there be good fellows
in the world, an a man could light on them, would take
her with all faults, and money enough.

GREMIO

I cannot tell. But I had as lief take her dowry with this
condition: to be whipp'd at the high cross every morning.

GREMIO

You can go to the devil's mother. Your virtues are so great that no one here will try to stop you. Their love is not so important, Hortensio, that we may bide our time and endure this dry spell. Our dough hasn't risen. Goodbye. Still, for the love I hold for my sweet Bianca, if I can find somewhere a proper man to teach 110 her the subjects she loves, I'll recommend him to her father.

HORTENSIO

I'll do that, too, Signor Gremio. But I beg a word with you. Though due to the reason for our quarrel, we've never yet consulted one another, you should realize, after careful consideration, that it concerns both of us—so that we can 115 again court our fair lady and be happy rivals for Bianca's love—to try to get one thing done above all.

GREMIO

What's that?

HORTENSIO

Indeed, sir, to get a husband for her sister.

GREMIO

A husband! You mean a devil. 120

HORTENSIO

I say "a husband."

GREMIO

And I say "a devil." Think, Hortensio—though her father is very rich, wouldn't a man have to be a complete idiot to agree to such a hellish marriage?

HORTENSIO

Nonsense, Gremio! Though it's beyond your patience and mine to endure her rudeness, there are many good fellows in 125 the world, if you could just find them, who would take her with all her faults and big fortune.

GREMIO

I can't say. But I'd just as soon take her dowry with this condition—to be whipped in the marketplace every morning.

HORTENSIO

130 Faith, as you say, there's small choice in rotten apples. But come, since this bar in law makes us friends, it shall be so far forth friendly maintain'd till by helping Baptista's eldest daughter to a husband we set his youngest free for a husband, and then have to 't afresh. Sweet Bianca! Happy

135 man be his dole! He that runs fastest gets the ring. How say you, Signior Gremio?

GREMIO

I am agreed; and would I had given him the best horse in Padua to begin his wooing that would thoroughly woo her, wed her and bed her, and rid the house of her! Come on.

[*Exit* GREMIO *and* HORTENSIO.]

TRANIO

140 I pray, sir, tell me, is it possible
That love should of a sudden take such hold?

LUCENTIO

O Tranio, till I found it to be true,
I never thought it possible or likely.
But see, while idly I stood looking on,

145 I found the effect of love-in-idleness;*
And now in plainness do confess to thee,
That art to me as secret and as dear
As Anna* to the Queen of Carthage was:
Tranio, I burn, I pine, I perish, Tranio,

150 If I achieve not this young modest girl.
Counsel me, Tranio, for I know thou canst;
Assist me, Tranio, for I know thou wilt.

TRANIO

Master, it is no time to chide you now;
Affection is not rated from the heart.

155 If love have touch'd you, naught remains but so:
"Redime te captum quam queas minimo."

---

145 *love-in-idleness* also is a name for the pansy, which was believed to spark love

148 *Anna* sister and confidante to Dido, Queen of Carthage

HORTENSIO

Well, as you say, there's little to choose from among rotten 130
apples. But come; since this restriction makes us friends, we'll
remain friends just until we can get Baptista's oldest daughter
a husband, thereby making the youngest free to marry, and
then resume our old rivalry. Sweet Bianca! May the winner be
rewarded with happiness! The fastest runner gets the prize. 135
What do you say, Signor Gremio?

GREMIO

I agree. And I'd give the man the best horse in Padua who
would begin courting her and who will really court her, marry
her, take her to bed, and get her out of this house. Come on.

> GREMIO and HORTENSIO exit.

TRANIO

Sir, tell me, is it possible 140
that you should fall in love so suddenly?

LUCENTIO

Oh Tranio! Until I discovered it does happen,
I never believed it was possible or even likely.
But while I stood by, idly watching,
I discovered how strong love-in-idleness is. 145
And now I'll plainly confess to you—
you who are as much in my confidence and as much my friend
as Anna was to the Queen of Carthage—
Tranio, I'll burn, I'll waste away, I'll die, Tranio,
if I don't win the hand of this sweet young girl. 150
Advise me, Tranio; I know you can.
Help me, Tranio; I know you will.

TRANIO

Master, it isn't the time to scold you, now.
Affection can't be scolded away.
If you're in love, there's nothing left to do except this: 155
"Buy your way out of captivity as cheaply as you can."

LUCENTIO

Gramercies, lad, go forward; this contents.
The rest will comfort, for thy counsel's sound.

TRANIO

Master, you look'd so longly on the maid,
160 Perhaps you mark'd not what's the pith of all.

LUCENTIO

O yes, I saw sweet beauty in her face,
Such as the daughter of Agenor* had,
That made great Jove to humble him to her hand,
When with his knees he kiss'd the Cretan strand.

TRANIO

165 Saw you no more? Mark'd you not how her sister
Began to scold and raise up such a storm
That mortal ears might hardly endure the din?

LUCENTIO

Tranio, I saw her coral lips to move
And with her breath she did perfume the air.
170 Sacred and sweet was all I saw in her.

TRANIO [*aside*]

Nay, then, 'tis time to stir him from his trance.—
I pray, awake, sir! If you love the maid,
Bend thoughts and wits to achieve her. Thus it stands:
Her elder sister is so curst and shrewd
175 That till the father rid his hands of her,
Master, your love must live a maid at home;
And therefore has he closely mew'd her up,
Because she will not be annoy'd with suitors.

LUCENTIO

Ah, Tranio, what a cruel father's he!
180 But art thou not advis'd, he took some care
To get her cunning schoolmasters to instruct her?

TRANIO

Ay, marry, am I, sir—and now 'tis plotted.

LUCENTIO

I have it, Tranio.

---

162 *daughter of Agenor* Europa, beloved by Jove, chief Roman god

LUCENTIO

Thanks very much, lad. Go on. This is soothing advice.
Your words will comfort me because your advice is good.

TRANIO

Master, you stared so longingly at the girl's face
that perhaps you didn't hear the gist of their conversation.   160

LUCENTIO

O yes, I saw the sweet beauty of her face.
She's just as beautiful as Agenor's daughter,
who so humbled mighty Jove
that he knelt on the shore of Crete before her.

TRANIO

Didn't you see anything else? Didn't you notice how her sister   165
began to scold and kick up such a fuss
that a human ear could scarcely stand the noise?

LUCENTIO

Tranio, I saw her coral lips move
and noticed how her breath perfumed the air.
Everything I saw about her was sacred and sweet.   170

TRANIO (*aside*)

I see it's time to rouse him up from this daze.
Please, sir, wake up. If you love the girl,
put your mind and wits to winning her. The situation is this:
her older sister is so testy and shrewish
that, until her father gets her off his hands,   175
Master, your beloved must remain at home, unmarried.
Therefore, her father is carefully guarding her
so that she won't be pestered by suitors.

LUCENTIO

Ah, Tranio, what a cruel father he is!
But didn't you hear that he wanted   180
to get some knowledgeable teachers to teach her?

TRANIO

Yes, certainly I know that, sir—ah, now I've got a plan!

LUCENTIO

I have one, too, Tranio.

TRANIO
                        Master, for my hand,
Both our inventions meet and jump in one.

LUCENTIO
Tell me thine first.

TRANIO
                        You will be schoolmaster
And undertake the teaching of the maid:
That's your device.

LUCENTIO
                        It is; may it be done?

TRANIO
Not possible; for who shall bear your part
And be in Padua here Vincentio's son,
Keep house, and ply his book, welcome his friends,
Visit his countrymen and banquet them?

LUCENTIO
*Basta,** content thee, for I have it full.
We have not yet been seen in any house,
Nor can we be distinguish'd by our faces
For man or master. Then it follows thus:
Thou shalt be master, Tranio, in my stead,
Keep house and port and servants, as I should.
I will some other be, some Florentine,
Some Neapolitan, or meaner man of Pisa.
'Tis hatch'd and shall be so. Tranio, at once
Uncase thee; take my colour'd* hat and cloak.

[They exchange clothes.]

When Biondello comes, he waits on thee;
But I will charm him first to keep his tongue.

185

190

195

200

205

---

195   *Basta* Italian for "enough!"

204   *colour'd* servants dressed in dark blue clothes, while their masters wore more
colorful clothing

TRANIO
Master, I'll bet
that both our schemes are the same.   185

LUCENTIO
Tell me yours first.

TRANIO
You'll be a teacher
and accept the job of teaching the girl—
that's your plan.

LUCENTIO
That's it; do you think we can manage it?   190

TRANIO
It won't work. Who will act your part
and play Vincentio's son here in Padua,
entertain, study his books, greet friends,
visit his countrymen, and invite them to dinner?

LUCENTIO
Enough. Rest easy. I've got it all planned.   195
No one knows who we are yet,
and no one can tell from our faces
who is servant and who is master. So my plan is this:
Tranio, you will play the master in my place,
keeping house, my style of living, and my servants, just as I
    would.   200
I'll become someone else—some Florentine,
or Neapolitan, or low-ranked man from Pisa.
That's the plan and we'll carry it out. Tranio, take off your
    clothes
immediately. Take my colorful hat and cloak.

    They switch clothes.

When Biondello arrives, he must serve you.   205
But first, I'll convince him to hold his tongue.

TRANIO
So had you need.
In brief, sir, sith it your pleasure is,
And I am tied to be obedient—
210   For so your father charg'd me at our parting,
"Be serviceable to my son," quoth he,
Although I think 'twas in another sense—
I am content to be Lucentio,
Because so well I love Lucentio.

LUCENTIO
215   Tranio, be so, because Lucentio loves;
And let me be a slave, t' achieve that maid
Whose sudden sight hath thrall'd my wounded eye.*

          Enter BIONDELLO.

Here comes the rogue.—Sirrah where have you been?

BIONDELLO
Where have I been? Nay, how now! Where are you?
220   Master, has my fellow Tranio stol'n your clothes? Or you
stol'n his? Or both? Pray, what's the news?

LUCENTIO
Sirrah, come hither; 'tis no time to jest,
And therefore frame your manners to the time.
Your fellow Tranio here, to save my life,
225   Puts my apparel and my count'nance on,
And I for my escape have put on his;
For in a quarrel since I came ashore
I kill'd a man and fear I was descried.
Wait you on him, I charge you, as becomes,
230   While I make way from hence to save my life.
You understand me?

BIONDELLO
                    Ay, sir! [*aside*] Ne'er a whit.

LUCENTIO
And not a jot of "Tranio" in your mouth.
Tranio is chang'd into Lucentio.

---

217   *wounded eye* pierced by Cupid's love arrow

TRANIO

Yes, you'd better.
In short, sir, since you want it this way,
and I'm bound to obey you—
for your father said to me when we left: 210
"Serve my son well," he said,
although I think he meant something different from this—
I'm willing to pretend I'm Lucentio
because I love Lucentio so much.

LUCENTIO

Do that, Tranio, because Lucentio is in love.   215
Let me play the servant in order to win the girl
who, after just a short glimpse, has captured my wounded eye.

      BIONDELLO *enters.*

Here comes the rascal. Where have you been, servant?

BIONDELLO

Where have I been! Wait, what's this? Where have you gone?
Master, has my fellow servant Tranio stolen your clothes, or have 220
you stolen his? Or both? Please, what's going on?

LUCENTIO

Servant, come here. This is no time for joking,
so match your behavior to the circumstances.
Your fellow servant Tranio, in order to save my life,
has put on my clothes and adopted my style.   225
And, so that I could escape, I put on his clothes.
I'm doing this because, in a quarrel that I had after coming
    ashore,
I killed a man, and I'm afraid that I was recognized.
So, I order you to serve Tranio as is proper,
while I escape from here in order to save my life.   230
Do you understand me?

BIONDELLO

Yes, sir! (*aside*) Not a bit.

LUCENTIO

And not a syllable of Tranio's name from you.
Tranio has become Lucentio.

BIONDELLO

235   The better for him. Would I were so too!

TRANIO

So could I, faith, boy, to have the next wish after,
That Lucentio indeed had Baptista's youngest daughter.
But, sirrah, not for my sake, but your master's, I advise
You use your manners discreetly in all kind of companies.

240   When I am alone, why, then I am Tranio;
But in all places else, your master Lucentio.

LUCENTIO

Tranio, let's go. One thing more rests, that thyself execute,
to make one among these wooers. If thou ask me why,
sufficeth my reasons are both good and weighty.

[Exeunt.]

The Presenters above speak.

1. SERVANT

245   My lord, you nod; you do not mind the play.

SLY

Yes, by Saint Anne, do I. A good matter, surely. Comes
there any more of it?

PAGE [*as* LADY]

My lord, 'tis but begun.

SLY

'Tis a very excellent piece of work, madam lady; would

250   'twere done!

They sit and mark.

BIONDELLO

Lucky him; I wish the same thing had happened to me! 235

TRANIO

I could wish that, too, boy, if I could have the next wish after that: that Lucentio really had Baptista's youngest daughter. But, servant, not for my sake but your master's, I advise you to be polite and discreet in everyone's company. When we're alone, then address me as Tranio, but everywhere else, I'm 240 your master Lucentio.

LUCENTIO

Let's go, Tranio. One other thing remains for you to do—you must join the prospective husbands. If you want to know why I ask this, be content with knowing that I have good and important reasons.

They exit.

The actors above speak.

FIRST SERVANT

My lord, you're dozing. You're not paying attention to the play. 245

SLY

Yes I am, by Saint Anne. It's good stuff, really; is there any more of it?

PAGE, *as* LADY

My lord, it's just started.

SLY

It's a very excellent piece of work, my lady; I wish it were over! 250

They sit and watch.

ACT I, SCENE II

[*Padua. Before Hortensio's house.*] *Enter* PETRUCHIO *and his man* GRUMIO.

PETRUCHIO

Verona, for a while I take my leave
To see my friends in Padua, but of all
My best beloved and approved friend,
Hortensio; and I trow this is his house.
5   Here, sirrah Grumio; knock, I say.

GRUMIO

Knock, sir? Whom should I knock? Is there any man has
rebus'd* your Worship?

PETRUCHIO

Villain, I say, knock me here soundly.

GRUMIO

Knock you here, sir? Why, sir, what am I, sir, that I should
10   knock you here, sir?

PETRUCHIO

Villain, I say, knock me at this gate
And rap me well, or I'll knock your knave's pate.

GRUMIO

My master is grown quarrelsome. I should knock you first,
And then I know after who comes by the worst.

PETRUCHIO

15   Will it not be?
Faith, sirrah, an you'll not knock, I'll ring it.*
I'll try how you can *sol, fa,* and sing it.

      He wrings him by the ears. [GRUMIO *falls.*]

GRUMIO

Help, mistress, help! My master is mad.

---

7   *rebused* Grumio really means "abused." He is using a malapropism—an unintentionally comic misuse of a word.

16 *ring it* Petruchio means he'll "wring" Grumio's neck.

ACT 1, SCENE 2

Padua, before Hortensio's house. PETRUCHIO *and his servant* GRUMIO *enter.*

PETRUCHIO
I've left Verona for a little while
to see my friends in Padua, especially
my best and proven friend,
Hortensio. I believe this is his house.
Here, my servant Grumio. Knock, I tell you.   5

GRUMIO
Knock, sir? Whom should I hit? Has someone rebused you,
your Worship?

PETRUCHIO
Rascal, I told you, knock here firmly.

GRUMIO
Knock here firmly? Why, sir, who am I, sir, that I should hit you
here, sir?   10

PETRUCHIO
Rascal, I said knock for me here at this door
and hit well, or I'll hit your foolish head.

GRUMIO
My master has become angry. If I hit you first,
I know who will be beaten for it afterwards.

PETRUCHIO
So you won't do it?   15
I'll tell you then, servant, if you don't knock, I'll ring it.
I'll see if you can sing your scales.

He wrings GRUMIO *by the ears.*

GRUMIO
Help, somebody, help! My master is mad.

PETRUCHIO

Now, knock when I bid you, sirrah villain!

Enter HORTENSIO.

HORTENSIO

20   How now, what's the matter? My old friend Grumio and
my good friend Petruchio? How do you all at Verona?

PETRUCHIO

Signior Hortensio, come you to part the fray?
Con tutto il cuore, ben trovato, * may I say.

HORTENSIO

Alla nostra casa ben venuto, molto honorato signor mio
25   *Petruchio.*
Rise, Grumio, rise; we will compound this quarrel.

GRUMIO

Nay, 'tis no matter, sir, what he 'leges in Latin. If this be
not a lawful cause for me to leave his service—look you, sir.
He bid me knock him and rap him soundly, sir. Well, was
30   it fit for a servant to use his master so, being perhaps, for
aught I see, two and thirty, a pip out?*
Whom, would to God, I had well knock'd at first,
Then had not Grumio come by the worst.

PETRUCHIO

A senseless villain, good Hortensio,
35   I bade the rascal knock upon your gate
And could not get him for my heart to do it.

GRUMIO

Knock at the gate? O heavens! Spake you not these words
plain, "Sirrah, knock me here, rap me here, knock me
well, and knock me soundly"? And come you now with
40   "knocking at the gate"?

---

23   *Con . . . trovato* Italian for "Well found (Welcome) will all my heart"

31   *two and thirty, a pip out* alludes to a card game (pip being a marking on a card)

PETRUCHIO

Now knock when I tell you to, you rascally servant.

HORTENSIO enters.

HORTENSIO

Why, what's the matter? My old friend Grumio! And my good[20] friend Petruchio! How is everyone in Verona?

PETRUCHIO

Signor Hortensio, did you come to settle the quarrel?
With all my heart, may I say that you are welcome.

HORTENSIO

Welcome to my house, my most honored Signor Petruchio. [25]
Get up, Grumio, get up. I'll settle this quarrel.

GRUMIO

It doesn't matter, sir, what he claims in Latin. If this isn't a legal reason to leave his service—Look, sir, he told me to knock him and hit him firmly. Well, is it proper for a servant to treat his [30] master like that when, perhaps for all that I know, he's out of his head?
I wish to God that I had hit him good.
Then I would not have suffered.

PETRUCHIO

What a stupid rascal! Good Hortensio,
I told the rascal to knock on your door [35]
and couldn't get him to do it on my life!

GRUMIO

Knock at the door? Oh heavens! Didn't you say these words quite clearly, "Servant, hit me here, rap here, knock well, and knock me firmly?" And now you're saying "knocking at the door"? [40]

PETRUCHIO

Sirrah, begone, or talk not, I advise you.

HORTENSIO

Petruchio, patience; I am Grumio's pledge.
Why, this's a heavy chance 'twixt him and you,
Your ancient, trusty, pleasant servant Grumio.
45 And tell me now, sweet friend, what happy gale
Blows you to Padua here from old Verona?

PETRUCHIO

Such wind as scatters young men through the world
To seek their fortunes farther than at home
Where small experience grows. But in a few,
50 Signior Hortensio, thus it stands with me:
Antonio, my father, is deceas'd;
And I have thrust myself into this maze,
Happily to wive and thrive as best I may.
Crowns in my purse I have and goods at home,
55 And so am come abroad to see the world.

HORTENSIO

Petruchio, shall I then come roundly to thee
And wish thee to a shrewd ill-favour'd wife?
Thou'dst thank me but a little for my counsel;
And yet I'll promise thee she shall be rich,
60 And very rich. But thou'rt too much my friend,
And I'll not wish thee to her.

PETRUCHIO

Signior Hortensio, 'twixt such friends as we
Few words suffice; and therefore, if thou know
One rich enough to be Petruchio's wife,
65 As wealth is burden of my wooing dance,
Be she as foul as was Florentius's love,*
As old as Sibyl,* and as curst and shrewd
As Socrates' Xanthippe,* or a worse,

---

66 *Florentius's love* Florentius is a fictional character who swore he would marry an
ugly woman if she answered a riddle that would save him from death.

67 *Sibyl* a seeress from Greek and Roman myths who lived to a very ancient age

68 *Socrates' Xanthippe* Socrates's wife, who was supposedly a shrew

PETRUCHIO

Servant, leave or shut up, I'm warning you.

HORTENSIO

Petruchio, please be patient. I'll swear by Grumio.
Why, this is an unhappy turn of events between you and him,
your longtime, trusted, pleasant servant Grumio.
So, tell me now, good friend, what fortunate wind   45
blows you here to Padua from old Verona?

PETRUCHIO

The kind of wind that scatters men throughout the world
to seek their fortunes away from home,
where little experience is gained. But, in short,
Signor Hortensio, this is my situation: 50
my father, Antonio, is dead,
and I've jumped onto this unknown path—
with any luck to marry and live as best as I can.
I have money in my purse and goods at home,
so I came abroad to see the world.   55

HORTENSIO

Petruchio, shall I be frank with you
and recommend you to a shrewish, unsuitable wife?
You'll thank me very little for my advice.
And yet, I'll guarantee you, she'll be rich,
very rich. But you're too good a friend,   60
and I won't recommend her to you.

PETRUCHIO

Signor Hortensio, friends like we two
understand each other without long explanations. So, if you
    know
someone rich enough to be my wife—
since wealth is the tune for my wedding dance—   65
if my bride is as ugly as Florentius's lover,
as old as Sibyl, as mean and shrewish
as Socrates's Xanthippe, or even worse,

She moves me not, or not removes at least
70 Affection's edge in me, were she as rough
As are the swelling Adriatic seas.
I come to wive it wealthily in Padua;
If wealthily, then happily in Padua.

GRUMIO [*to* HORTENSIO]
Nay, look you, sir, he tells you flatly what his mind is.
75 Why give him gold enough, and marry him to a puppet or
an aglet-baby,* or an old trot with ne'er a tooth in her
head, though she have as many diseases as two-and-fifty
horses. Why, nothing comes amiss, so money comes withal.

HORTENSIO
Petruchio, since we are stepp'd thus far in,
80 I will continue that I broach'd in jest.
I can, Petruchio, help thee to a wife
With wealth enough, and young and beauteous,
Brought up as best becomes a gentlewoman.
Her only fault, and that is faults enough,
85 Is that she is intolerable curst
And shrewd and froward, so beyond all measure
That, were my state far worser than it is,
I would not wed her for a mine of gold.

PETRUCHIO
Hortensio, peace! Thou know'st not gold's effect.
90 Tell me her father's name and 'tis enough;
For I will board her, though she chide as loud
As thunder when the clouds in autumn crack.

HORTENSIO
Her father is Baptista Minola,
An affable and courteous gentleman.
95 Her name is Katherina Minola,
Renown'd in Padua for her scolding tongue.

PETRUCHIO
I know her father, though I know not her;
And he knew my deceased father well.
I will not sleep, Hortensio, till I see her;

---

76 *aglet-baby* the figure of a woman on the tip of a lace

I won't be bothered, and my
affections won't be dulled at all, even if she were as rough   70
as the stormy Adriatic sea.
I've come to Padua to marry a rich woman.
If I marry richly, then I'll live happily in Padua.

GRUMIO [*to* HORTENSIO]
You see, sir, he tells you plainly how he feels. Just give him
enough money, and then marry him to a doll or a lace-tip or   75
an old hag without a tooth in her head, even if she has as
many diseases as fifty-two horses. Well, everything's fine if
money goes with it.

HORTENSIO
Petruchio, since we've gone this far,
I'll tell you more of what I first said as a joke.   80
I can show you, Petruchio, where to get a wife
who is rich, young, beautiful,
and raised like a lady should be.
Her only fault—and it's a big enough fault—
is that she is intolerably mean   85
and shrewish and stubborn—beyond all comparison—
so that even if my income were much less than it is,
I wouldn't marry her for a gold mine!

PETRUCHIO
Enough, Hortensio! You don't know the power of gold.
Tell me what her father's name is—that will do.   90
For I'll court her even if she scolds as loud
as when, in autumn, thunder makes the clouds crack.

HORTENSIO
Her father is Baptista Minola.
He's a friendly and courteous gentleman.
The woman's name is Katherine Minola,   95
famous throughout Padua for her scolding tongue.

PETRUCHIO
I know her father, though I don't know her.
And Baptista knew my dead father well.
I won't sleep, Hortensio, until I've seen her,

And therefore let me be thus bold with you
To give you over at this first encounter,
Unless you will accompany me thither.

GRUMIO

I pray you, sir, let him go while the humour lasts. O' my
word, an she knew him as well as I do, she would think
scolding would do little good upon him. She may
perhaps call him half a score knaves or so. Why, that's
nothing. An he begin once, he'll rail in his rope tricks.* I'll
tell you what, sir, an she stand him but a little, he will
throw a figure in her face and so disfigure her with it that
she shall have no more eyes to see withal than a cat. You
know him not, sir.

HORTENSIO

Tarry, Petruchio, I must go with thee,
For in Baptista's keep my treasure is.
He hath the jewel of my life in hold,
His youngest daughter, beautiful Bianca,
And her withholds from me and other more,
Suitors to her and rivals in my love,
Supposing it a thing impossible,
For those defects I have before rehears'd,
That ever Katherina will be woo'd.
Therefore this order hath Baptista ta'en,
That none shall have access unto Bianca
Till Katherine the curst have got a husband.

GRUMIO

"Katherine the curst!"
A title for a maid, of all titles the worst.

HORTENSIO

Now shall my friend Petruchio do me grace,
And offer me disguis'd in sober robes
To old Baptista as a schoolmaster
Well seen in music, to instruct Bianca;
That so I may, by this device at least,
Have leave and leisure to make love to her
And unsuspected court her by herself.

---

107 *rope tricks* means "rhetoric" and plays on the word "figure," as in figure of speech
and "roguish behavior"

72   *The Taming of the Shrew*

so let me be so bold as $\qquad$ 100
to leave you now, though it is our first meeting—
unless you want to go there with me.

GRUMIO

I beg you, sir, let him go while he's still in the mood. Really, if
she knew him as well as I do, she'd think scolding would have $\quad$ 105
little effect on him. She might call him half a dozen rascals or
something like that. It wouldn't bother him. Just start him off,
and he'll rant and rave. I'll tell you, sir, if she's just a little
obstinate, he'll spit a figure of speech at her and hurt her so
much that she'll be as blind as a cat. You don't know him, sir. $\quad$ 110

HORTENSIO

Wait a minute, Petruchio, I must go with you
because my treasure is in Baptista's house.
He has the jewel of my life in his stronghold—
his youngest daughter, the beautiful Bianca. $\qquad$ 115
He keeps me away from her, and others—
her suitors and my rivals—
since he thinks it is impossible,
because of those faults I've told you about,
that Katherine will ever be married. $\qquad$ 120
So Baptista's given this order:
no one will see or talk to Bianca
until Katherine the shrew has a husband.

GRUMIO

"Katherine the shrew!"
That's the worst possible nickname for a woman. $\qquad$ 125

HORTENSIO

Now my friend, Petruchio, do me a favor
and introduce me—after I've disguised myself in proper
    clothing—
to old Baptista as a teacher
well-versed in music and able to teach Bianca.
By this little scheme, I can at least $\qquad$ 130
be given permission to see her and time to win her
and court her without suspicion when we're alone.

GRUMIO

Here's no knavery! See, to beguile the old folks, how the
young folks lay their heads together!

Enter GREMIO *and* LUCENTIO, *disguised [as
CAMBIO, a schoolmaster.]*

135   Master, master, look about you! Who goes there, ha!

HORTENSIO

Peace, Grumio! It is the rival of my love.
Petruchio, stand by awhile.

*[PETRUCIO, HORTENSIO, and GREMIO stand
aside.]*

GRUMIO *[aside]*

A proper stripling, and an amorous!

GREMIO *[to LUCENTIO]*

O, very well; I have **perus'd** the note.
140   Hark you, sir, I'll have them very fairly bound,
All books of love. See that at any hand;
And see you read no other lectures to her.
You understand me? Over and beside
Signior Baptista's liberality,
145   I'll mend it with a **largess**. Take your paper too;
And let me have them very well perfum'd,
For she is sweeter than perfume itself
To whom they go to. What will you read to her?

LUCENTIO *[as CAMBIO]*

Whate'er I read to her, I'll plead for you
150   As for my patron, stand you so assur'd,
As firmly as yourself were still in place;
Yea, and perhaps with more successful words
Than you, unless you were a scholar, sir.

GREMIO

O this learning, what a thing it is!

GRUMIO *[aside]*

155   O this woodcock, what an ass it is!

PETRUCHIO *[aside]*

Peace, sirrah!

GRUMIO (*sarcastically*)
Why, this is honest stuff! See how the young
folks put their heads together to fool the old folks.

GREMIO *and* LUCENTIO, *who is disguised as* CAMBIO, *enter.*

Master, master—look! Who's that? 135

HORTENSIO
Quiet, Grumio! That's my rival for Bianca's love.
Petruchio, stand close by for a moment.

GRUMIO (*looking at* GREMIO, *exclaims sarcastically*)
He's a handsome boy and a real lover!

GREMIO (*to* LUCENTIO)
Very well, I've read the reading list.
Listen, sir, I want all the books to have pretty covers. 140
And all the books must be about love. That's important.
See that you don't talk to her about anything else.
I think you understand me. Besides
Signor Baptista's good wages,
I'll add on a gift. Take the list, too. 145
I'll see that the sheets are nicely perfumed
since she is sweeter than perfume itself—
the girl they're going to. What will you read to her?

LUCENTIO, as CAMBIO
Whatever I read to her, I'll court her for you,
my patron—you can be as certain of that 150
as if you yourself were still present.
Yes, I'll do that and perhaps with more winning words
than you would use, unless you were a scholar, sir.

GREMIO
Oh, knowledge is a wonderful thing!

GRUMIO (*aside*)
Oh, this fool is such an ass! 155

PETRUCHIO
Quiet, servant!

HORTENSIO [*aside*]

Grumio, mum! [*Coming forward*]

        God save you, Signior Gremio.

GREMIO

And you are well met, Signior Hortensio.

160 Trow you whither I am going? To Baptista Minola.

I promis'd to enquire carefully

About a schoolmaster for the fair Bianca;

And by good fortune I have lighted well

On this young man, for learning and behaviour

165 Fit for her turn, well read in poetry

And other books—good ones, I warrant ye.

HORTENSIO

'Tis well. And I have met a gentleman

Hath promis'd me to help me to another,

A fine musician, to instruct our mistress;

170 So shall I no whit be behind in duty

To fair Bianca, so belov'd of me.

GREMIO

Belov'd of me, and that my deeds shall prove.

GRUMIO [*aside*]

And that his bags shall prove.

HORTENSIO

Gremio, 'tis now no time to vent our love.

175 Listen to me, and if you speak me fair,

I'll tell you news indifferent good for either.

Here is a gentleman whom by chance I met,

Upon agreement* from us to his liking,

Will undertake to woo curst Katherine,

180 Yea, and to marry her, if her dowry please.

GREMIO

So said, so done, is well.

Hortensio, have you told him all her faults?

---

178   *agreement* Hortensio means Petruchio will court Kate if the expenses he incurs while wooing her are paid.

HORTENSIO
Grumio, hush! (*coming forward*)
Good day to you, Signor Gremio!

GREMIO
Nice to see you, Signor Hortensio.
So you know where I'm going? To Baptista Minola.   160
I promised to search
for a schoolmaster for beautiful Bianca,
and with good luck, I happened to find
this young man. In knowledge and bearing
he's exactly right for her. He's well-read in poetry   165
and other books—good ones, too, I'll bet.

HORTENSIO
That's good. I've met a gentleman, too,
who has promised me to help find a teacher—
a fine musician who can teach our lady love—
so I won't be lagging in my duty   170
to beautiful Bianca, my dearly beloved.

GREMIO
My dearly beloved—my actions will prove that.

GRUMIO (*aside*)
And his moneybags will prove that.

HORTENSIO
Gremio, this isn't the time to talk about our love.
Listen to me, and if you're being honest with me,   175
I'll tell you some news that's good for us both.

     Presents PETRUCHIO.

Here is a gentleman whom I met by chance.
If we agree to what he asks,
he says he'll try to court the shrewish Katherine—
yes, even marry her if he likes her dowry.   180

GREMIO
If he does as he says, that would be good.
Hortensio, have you told him about all her faults?

PETRUCHIO

I know she is an irksome, brawling scold.
If that be all, masters, I hear no harm.

GREMIO

185   No? Say'st me so, friend? What countryman?

PETRUCHIO

Born in Verona, old Antonio's son.
My father dead, my fortune lives for me;
And I do hope good days and long to see.

GREMIO

O sir, such a life with such a wife, were strange!
190   But if you have a stomach, to 't i' God's name;
You shall have me assisting you in all.
But will you woo this wildcat?

PETRUCHIO

Will I live?

GRUMIO [*aside*]

Will he woo her? Ay, or I'll hang her.

PETRUCHIO

195   Why came I hither but to that intent?
Think you a little din can daunt mine ears?
Have I not in my time heard lions roar?
Have I not heard the sea, puff'd up with winds,
Rage like an angry boar chafed with sweat?
200   Have I not heard great ordnance in the field,
And heaven's artillery thunder in the skies?
Have I not in a pitched battle heard
Loud 'larums, neighing steeds, and trumpets clang?
And do you tell me of a woman's tongue,
205   That gives not half so great a blow to hear
As will a chestnut in a farmer's fire?
Tush, tush, fear boys with bugs!

GRUMIO [*aside*]

For he fears none.

GREMIO

Hortensio, hark.
210   This gentleman is happily arriv'd,
My mind presumes, for his own good and yours.

PETRUCHIO

I know she's an irritating, quarrelsome shrew.
If that's all, gentlemen, I'm not discouraged.

GREMIO

No! You really mean that, my friend? Where are you from?   185

PETRUCHIO

I was born in Verona. I'm old Antonio's son.
My father is dead now, my fortune still is to be made,
and I hope to live a good, long life.

GREMIO

Oh, sir, such a life with such a wife is most unlikely!
But if you have the desire to try, go to it, by God.   190
I'll help you in every possible way.
But will you really court this wildcat?

PETRUCHIO

Will I live?

GRUMIO (*aside*)

Listen to him—will he court her? Yes, or I'll hang her.

PETRUCHIO

Why did I come here except to do that?   195
Do you think a little noise can frighten me?
Haven't I heard lions roaring in my day?
Haven't I heard the sea, swelled by winds,
rage like a hot, angry boar?
Haven't I heard the big cannons in battles   200
and heaven's gunfire thunder in the skies?
Haven't I heard in the heat of battle
the call to arms, neighing horses, and the clang of trumpets?
And you tell me about a woman's sharp tongue
that doesn't sound as half as loud   205
as a chestnut cracking in a farmer's fire?
Nonsense, nonsense. Go frighten boys with goblins.

GRUMIO (*aside*)

Because they don't scare him.

GREMIO

Listen, Hortensio,
this gentleman has arrived at a good moment,   210
I think—both for us and for him.

HORTENSIO
I promis'd we would be contributors
And bear his charge of wooing whatsoe'er.

GREMIO
And so we will, provided that he win her.

GRUMIO [*aside*]
215   I would I were as sure of a good dinner.

>   *Enter* TRANIO [*disguised as* LUCENTIO] *and*
>   BIONDELLO.

TRANIO [*as* LUCENTIO]
Gentlemen, God save you. If I may be bold,
Tell me, I beseech you, which is the readiest way
To the house of Signior Baptista Minola?

BIONDELLO
He that has the two fair daughters? Is 't he you mean?

TRANIO [*as* LUCENTIO]
220   Even he, Biondello.

GREMIO
Hark you, sir, you mean not her to—

TRANIO [*as* LUCENTIO]
Perhaps, him and her, sir. What have you to do?

PETRUCHIO
Not her that chides, sir, at any hand, I pray.

TRANIO [*as* LUCENTIO]
I love no chiders, sir. Biondello, let's away.

LUCENTIO [*aside*]
225   Well begun, Tranio.

HORTENSIO
                Sir, a word ere you go;
Are you a suitor to the maid you talk of, yea or no?

TRANIO [*as* LUCENTIO]
And if I be, sir, is it any offence?

HORTENSIO
I promised we would chip in
and pay the expenses for his courting, whatever the cost.

GREMIO
And we'll do just that, provided he marry her.

GRUMIO (*aside*)
I wish I were as sure of a good dinner.   215

> TRANIO (*as* LUCENTIO), *very well-dressed, and* BIONDELLO
> *enter.*

TRANIO, *as* LUCENTIO
Gentlemen, God bless you! If I may be so bold to ask,
please tell me which is the quickest way
to Signor Baptista Minola's house?

BIONDELLO
The man who has two lovely daughters—is that the one you
mean?

TRANIO, *as* LUCENTIO
That's the one, Biondello.   220

GREMIO
Listen, sir—the girl—you don't mean to—

TRANIO, *as* LUCENTIO
Perhaps the girl and Signor Baptista, sir. What business is it of
yours?

PETRUCHIO
You don't have any plans for the shrew, at any rate, I hope.

TRANIO, *as* LUCENTIO
I don't care for shrews, sir. Biondello, let's go.

LUCENTIO (*aside*)
That was a nice start, Tranio.   225

HORTENSIO
Sir, I'd like a word with you before you go:
Are you a suitor of the girl you spoke of—yes or no?

TRANIO, *as* LUCENTIO
And if I am a suitor, sir, is that a crime?

GREMIO

No; if without more words you will get you hence.

TRANIO [*as* LUCENTIO]

230   Why, sir, I pray, are not the streets as free
For me as for you?

GREMIO

But so is not she.

TRANIO [*as* LUCENTIO]

For what reason, I beseech you?

GREMIO

For this reason, if you'll know:
235   That she's the choice love of Signior Gremio.

HORTENSIO

That she's the chosen of Signior Hortensio.

TRANIO [*as* LUCENTIO]

Softly, my masters! If you be gentlemen,
Do me this right: hear me with patience.
Baptista is a noble gentleman
240   To whom my father is not all unknown;
And were his daughter fairer than she is,
She may more suitors have, and me for one.
Fair Leda's daughter* had a thousand wooers;
Then well one more may fair Bianca have;
245   And so she shall. Lucentio shall make one,
Though Paris came in hope to speed alone.

GREMIO

What! This gentleman will out-talk us all!

LUCENTIO [*as* CAMBIO]

Sir, give him head; I know he'll prove a jade.

PETRUCHIO

Hortensio, to what end are all these words?

HORTENSIO [*as* TRANIO]

250   Sir, let me be so bold as ask you,
Did you yet ever see Baptista's daughter?

---

243   *Leda's daughter* Helen, daughter of Leda and the Greek god Zeus. Paris took
Helen away from her husband to Troy, causing the Trojan War.

GREMIO
>No, not if you leave Padua without another word.

TRANIO, *as* LUCENTIO
>Why is that, sir? Aren't these streets just as free   230
>to me as they are to you?

GREMIO
>But not her.

TRANIO, *as* LUCENTIO
>Why, may I ask?

GREMIO
>For this reason, if you want to know:
>she's my chosen love.   235

HORTENSIO
>She's my chosen love!

TRANIO, *as* LUCENTIO
>Relax, gentlemen! If you're gentlemen,
>grant me this right—listen to me with patience.
>Baptista is a noble gentleman
>to whom my father is not a complete stranger.   240
>And if his daughter were lovelier than she is,
>she could still have more suitors—me for one.
>Lovely Leda's daughter had a thousand suitors.
>Then certainly lovely Bianca can have one more.
>And so she will. Lucentio will be one,   245
>even if Paris showed up, hoping to court her without rivals.

GREMIO
>Really! This gentleman will out-talk us all!

LUCENTIO, *as* CAMBIO
>Sir, let him talk. I know he'll fade in the stretch.

PETRUCHIO
>Hortensio, what's all the point to this talk?

HORTENSIO, *as* TRANIO
>Sir, let me be so bold as to ask you   250
>if you've ever seen Baptista's daughter?

TRANIO [*as* LUCENTIO]
    No, sir, but hear I do that he hath two,
    The one as famous for a scolding tongue
    As is the other for beauteous modesty.

PETRUCHIO
255   Sir, sir, the first's for me; let her go by.

GREMIO
    Yea, leave that labour to great Hercules,*
    And let it be more than Alcides's twelve.

PETRUCHIO [*to* TRANIO]
    Sir, understand you this of me, in sooth:
    The youngest daughter, whom you hearken for,
260   Her father keeps from all access of suitors
    And will not promise her to any man
    Until the elder sister first be wed.
    The younger then is free, and not before.

TRANIO [*as* LUCENTIO]
    If it be so, sir, that you are the man
265   Must stead us all, and me amongst the rest,
    And if you break the ice and do this feat,
    Achieve the elder, set the younger free
    For our access, whose hap shall be to have her
    Will not so graceless be to be **ingrate**.

HORTENSIO
270   Sir, you say well, and well you do conceive;
    And since you do profess to be a suitor,
    You must, as we do, gratify this gentleman,
    To whom we all rest generally beholding.

TRANIO [*as* LUCENTIO]
    Sir, I shall not be slack; in sign whereof,
275   Please ye we may contrive this afternoon
    And quaff carouses to our mistress's health;
    And do as adversaries do in law,
    Strive mightily, but eat and drink as friends.

---

256   *Hercules* or Alcides, a Greek hero, performed twelve great labors to free himself

TRANIO, *as* LUCENTIO
No, sir, but I hear that he has two daughters,
the one as renowned for her shrewish tongue
as the other one is for her beauty and modesty.

PETRUCHIO
Sir, the oldest daughter is mine; pass her by. 255

GREMIO
Yes, leave that labor to great Hercules, here.
That will amount to more that Alcides' twelve labors.

PETRUCHIO (*to* TRANIO)
Sir, understand this that I'll tell you honestly:
the youngest daughter, the one you're after,
is kept away from all suitors by her father, 260
who refuses to let any man marry her
until his eldest daughter is married first.
Then the younger one is free to marry, and only then.

TRANIO, *as* LUCENTIO
If that's so, sir, then you are the man
who must help us all—me included. 265
And if you break the ice and are able to
win the eldest daughter and set the younger one free
so we can court her, whoever is lucky enough to gain her love
will not be so ungracious as to be ungrateful.

HORTENSIO
Sir, that's well-spoken, and you state the situation well. 270
And since you say that you're a suitor,
you must, like us, reward this gentleman
to whom we all remain in debt.

TRANIO, *as* LUCENTIO
Sir, I won't duck my share—and to show you that I mean it,
if it suits you, let's spend the afternoon 275
drinking from deep-bottomed cups to our lady's health,
and do just as attorneys do:
try to beat the other fellow in court, but eat and drink like
    friends.

GRUMIO / BIONDELLO

O excellent motion! Fellows, let's be gone.

HORTENSIO

280   The motion's good indeed, and be it so.—
Petruchio, I shall be your *ben venuto.**

[*Exeunt.*]

---

281   *I . . . venuto.* I will make sure of your welcome.

GRUMIO and **BIONDELLO**

That's a wonderful idea! Gentlemen, let's go.

HORTENSIO

It's a good idea, and let's do it.   280
Petruchio, I'll be your host.

They exit.

Act I Review

Discussion Questions

1. What ideas about the play can you find in the Induction?

2. What do you think is the purpose of the practical joke the Lord plays on Sly in the Induction scenes?

3. Why do you think Shakespeare sets the Induction in England and the play itself in Italy?

4. What do you think Lucentio's opening speech reveals about his character?

5. What does Kate's first appearance immediately reveal about her character?

6. What is the relationship between Tranio and Lucentio?

7. Does Kate show any sign that she is conflicted about marriage?

8. Why does Baptista refuse to allow Bianca to marry before Kate?

Literary Elements

1. There are many **allusions**, or references to things outside the text, in Act I. Find some examples and explain what they refer to and how you think they add to the text.

2. **Foreshadowing** means clues or suggestions about later events in a plot. What examples of foreshadowing do you detect in Act I?

3. **Hyperbole** refers to obvious exaggeration. Look at Petruchio's speech in Act I, Scene ii, lines 195–207 ["Why came I hither . . ."]. Name all the examples of hyperbole you can find, and explain what you think this says about his character and motives.

4. **Imagery** refers to word pictures that appeal to the five senses and add emotion and power to the writing. Look again at Petruchio's speech in Act I, Scene ii, lines 195–207, and underline all of the images of noise and violence that you see there. What point is he trying to make?

Writing Prompts

1. Write a personals ad in Elizabethan English. Write it from the point of view of one of the male suitors, Lucentio or Petruchio, or from the perspective of Kate or Bianca.

2. Think about the Messenger's admonishment in the Induction: ". . . frame your mind to mirth and merriment, which bars a thousand harms and lengthens life." Do you think it is true that humor inoculates you against harm and extends your life? Write a short essay that supports or disputes this proposition.

3. In Shakespeare's time, schoolchildren kept track of expressions known as "commonplaces"—catchphrases that seemed to contain some truth. *The Taming of the Shrew*, like all of Shakespeare's plays, has many such pithy phrases, for example, "No profit grows where is no pleasure ta'en." Begin your own book of commonplaces by filling it with lines from the play that you find especially true or memorable.

4. Assume that you write an advice column for a newspaper or magazine. A modern-day Lucentio or Bianca writes to you asking for your advice. He or she explains the circumstances that have made it difficult to attain true love. First write his or her letter, and then write your response.

5. In a reference book about classical mythology, look up one of the lovers mentioned in Act I—Adonis, Daphne, or Apollo, for example. Write a paragraph summarizing the story of this character. Why do you think Shakespeare makes these classical allusions at this point in the story?

The Taming of the Shrew

ACT II

Erika Alexander as Bianca (foreground) and Allison Janney as Katherine,
Delacorte Theatre, 1999

*"...for you are call'd plain Kate, and
bonny Kate, and sometimes Kate the curst...
Kate of Kate Hall, my super-dainty Kate...."*

Before You Read

1. As you read, consider how Kate is characterized by others as well as by her own comments and actions.

2. Think about how different Kate is from her sister Bianca. How do you think this will serve the plot?

3. Kate and Petruchio, when left alone in this act, engage in a furious bout of wits. As you read, consider all that is expressed directly and all that is implied by their heated exchange. Decide whether you think one of them emerges the victor.

Literary Elements

1. A **pun** is a play on words that sound similar but have different spellings or meanings. In Act I of *The Taming of the Shrew*, Baptista tells two potential suitors to Kate that they may "court her" at their pleasure. Gremio responds, "To cart her, rather." In Shakespeare's time, unruly women were sometimes paraded in open carts to humiliate them.

2. A **simile** makes a comparison between two unlike things using *like* or *as*. Finding the drunken Christopher Sly passed out in the road, the Lord says, "how like a swine he lies!"

3. A **foil** is a character who makes a stark contrast to another character. In *The Taming of the Shrew*, Lucentio is a foil to Petruchio. Lucentio is well-mannered and gentle but conducts his courtship of Bianca deceptively. Petruchio, on the other hand, is ill-mannered and boisterous, but pursues Kate openly and aggressively.

4. **Irony** refers to the difference between appearance and reality. When introducing himself as a suitor to Kate, Petruchio asks Baptista, "Have you not a daughter / Call'd Katherina, fair and virtuous?" At this point, he is well aware that Kate is no model of virtue.

Words to Know

The following vocabulary words appear in Act II in the original text of Shakespeare's play. However, they are words that are still used today. Read the definitions here, and pay attention to the words as you read the play (they will be in boldfaced type).

cavil	quibble; nitpick
covenants	agreements; contracts
coy	shy; aloof
discomfited	out of sorts; uncomfortable
dissemble	lie; evade
eloquence	fluency; expressiveness
peremptory	dictatorial; arrogant
temperate	moderate; mild
volubility	talkativeness; chattiness
waning	weakening; diminishing

Act Summary

Kate is bullying Bianca when Baptista steps in and puts an end to it. Kate accuses him of favoring his younger daughter, and he accuses her of being a "devilish spirit."

Then the suitors to the two young women arrive: Gremio, Hortensio, and Petruchio. The latter announces that he wishes to have Kate's hand in marriage and suggests that Hortensio (disguised as Litio) be her music teacher. Gremio proposes that Lucentio (disguised as Cambio) teach Bianca languages.

Then Tranio, dressed as his master Lucentio, arrives. He bears gifts for Bianca, whom he declares he will woo (on Lucentio's behalf). Baptista accepts the tutors and gifts and also agrees that Petruchio may wed Kate, provided she falls in love with him.

Timothy Dalton as Petruchio and Vanessa Redgrave as Kate, Theatre Royal Haymarket, London, 1986

Hortensio announces that Kate has clobbered him with the lute he gave Bianca. Petruchio is much impressed and wants to meet Kate immediately. After everyone leaves, he describes his plans for "taming" her in a soliloquy.

Alone, Kate and Petruchio let fly their verbal daggers at each other. Petruchio overrides her objections to marrying him and pretends to her father that she has not only agreed but proved very affectionate. The wedding is planned for the following Sunday.

Baptista now is free to accept the wealthiest suitor's bid for Bianca's hand. Tranio—dressed as Lucentio still—declares that his father Vincentio's wealth is vast, so winning Bianca. Baptista wants to meet Vincentio first, however, to guarantee this wealth. After the men leave, Tranio decides to find a replacement for Vincentio so as to speed his master's plans along.

ACT II, SCENE I

[*Padua. A room in Baptista's house.*] *Enter* KATHERINE
and BIANCA [*with her hands tied*].

BIANCA

Good sister, wrong me not, nor wrong yourself,
To make a bondmaid and a slave of me.
That I disdain; but for these other goods, X
Unbind my hands, I'll pull them off myself, X

5　X Yea, all my raiment, to my petticoat;
Or what you will command me will I do,
So well I know my duty to my elders.

KATHERINE

Of all thy suitors here I charge thee tell
Whom thou lov'st best; see thou **dissemble** not.

BIANCA

10　X Believe me, sister, of all the men alive
I never yet beheld that special face
Which I could fancy more than any other.

KATHERINE

Minion, thou liest. Is 't not Hortensio?

BIANCA

If you affect him, sister, here I swear
15　I'll please for you myself, but you shall have him.

KATHERINE

O, then belike you fancy riches more.
You will have Gremio to keep you fair.

BIANCA

Is it for him you do envy me so?
Nay, then you jest, and now I well perceive
20　X You have but jested with me all this while.
　X I prithee, sister Kate, untie my hands.

KATHERINE

If that be jest, then all the rest was so.

[*Strikes her.*]

Enter BAPTISTA.

ACT 2, SCENE 1

Padua. A room in Baptista's house. KATHERINE *and* BIANCA, *with her hands tied, enter.*

BIANCA
Dear sister, don't abuse me or abuse yourself
by making me a servant and a slave.
I despise that. But as for these other ornaments,
untie my hands, and I'll pull them off myself.
Yes, all my clothing, down to my petticoat.   5
Or whatever you order me to do, I will,
to show you how well I know my duty to my elders.

KATHERINE
I demand that you tell me which one of all your suitors
you love best—and don't lie to me!

BIANCA
Believe me, sister, of all the men I've seen,   10
I've never yet seen that special face
that attracted me more than any other.

KATHERINE
You spoiled brat, you're lying! It's Hortensio, isn't it?

BIANCA
If you like him, sister, I swear here and now
that I'll try to win him for your husband.   15

KATHERINE
Oh, then perhaps you're more partial to wealth:
you'll marry Gremio to keep you pretty.

BIANCA
Is it because of him that you hate me so much?
No, you're joking. Now I see that
you've just been joking all this time.   20
Please, sister Kate, untie my hands.

KATHERINE
If this is a joke, then so was everything else.

Hits BIANCA.

BAPTISTA *enters.*

BAPTISTA

Why, how now, dame? Whence grows this insolence?—
Bianca, stand aside.—Poor girl,

25   she weeps! [*He unties her hands.*]
    ✕ Go ply thy needle; meddle not with her.
    [*to* KATHERINE] For shame, thou hilding of a devilish
          spirit!
    Why dost thou wrong her that did ne'er wrong thee?

30   When did she cross thee with a bitter word?

KATHERINE

Her silence flouts me, and I'll be reveng'd!

        [*Flies after* BIANCA.]

BAPTISTA

What, in my sight?—Bianca, get thee in.

        [*Exit* BIANCA.]

KATHERINE

✕ |What, will you not suffer me? Nay,| now I see
    She is your treasure, she must have a husband;

35   I must dance barefoot* on her wedding day
    And, for your love to her,| lead apes in hell.*| ✕
    Talk not to me; I will go sit and weep
    Till I can find occasion of revenge.

        [*Exit.*]

? **BAPTISTA**

Was ever gentleman thus griev'd as I?

40   But who comes here?

> *Enter* GREMIO, LUCENTIO [*disguised as* CAMBIO]
> *in the habit of a mean man;* PETRUCHIO *with*
> HORTENSIO [*disguised as* LITIO], *a musician; and*
> TRANIO [*disguised as* LUCENTIO], *with his boy,*
> BIONDELLO, *bearing a lute and books.*

GREMIO

Good morrow, neighbour Baptista.

---

35   *dance barefoot* Older unmarried sisters were expected to do this at the weddings
    of their younger sisters.

36   *lead apes in hell* proverbial fate of old maids

BAPTISTA

What's this, woman? What's the cause of this insolence?
Bianca, stand aside. Poor girl, she's crying! (*He unties her hands.*)   25
Go and do your sewing. Stay out of Katherine's way.
(*To* KATHERINE) Shame on you, you wretch, you devil!
Why do you hurt her when she's never hurt you?
When did she ever anger you with a bitter word?   30

KATHERINE

Her silence insults me, and I'll have my revenge!

    Runs after BIANCA.

BAPTISTA

What—before my very eyes? Bianca, hurry to your room.

    BIANCA *exits.*

KATHERINE

So, you try to stop me? Well, now I see
that she's your treasure. She must have a husband,
while I dance barefoot on her wedding day,   35
and on account of your love for her, I must lead apes in hell.
Don't speak to me! I'll go sit and cry
until I can find an opportunity for revenge.

    She exits.

BAPTISTA

Was there ever a man so faced with troubles as I am?
But who is this approaching?   40

    GREMIO; LUCENTIO, *disguised as* CAMBIO, *in the clothes
    of a lower-class man;* PETRUCHIO; HORTENSIO, *disguised
    as* LITIO, *a musician;* TRANIO, *disguised as* LUCENTIO; *and
    the servant* BIONDELLO, *carrying a lute and books, all enter.*

GREMIO

Good morning, neighbor Baptista.

BAPTISTA

Good morrow, neighbour Gremio.—\God save you,
gentlemen! X

PETRUCHIO

And you, good sir! Pray, have you not a daughter
45 Call'd Katherina, fair and virtuous?

BAPTISTA

I have a daughter, sir, call'd Katherina.

GREMIO [*to* PETRUCHIO]

X You are too blunt; go to it orderly.

PETRUCHIO

X You wrong me, Signior Gremio. Give me leave.—
I am a gentleman of Verona, sir,
50 That, hearing of her beauty and her wit,
Her affability and bashful modesty,
Her wondrous qualities and mild behaviour,
Am bold to show myself a forward guest
Within your house, to make mine eye the witness X
55 Of that report which I so oft have heard. X
And, for an entrance to my entertainment,
I do present you with a man of mine,

[*Presenting* HORTENSIO, disguised as LITIO]

Cunning in music and the mathematics,
To instruct her fully in those sciences,
60 X Whereof I know she is not ignorant.
X Accept of him, or else you do me wrong.
His name is Litio, born in Mantua.

BAPTISTA

You're welcome, sir; and he for your good sake.
But for my daughter Katherine, this I know,
65 She is not for your turn, the more my grief.

PETRUCHIO

I see you do not mean to part with her,
Or else you like not of my company.

BAPTISTA

Good morning, neighbor Gremio. Bless you, gentlemen!

PETRUCHIO

And you, too, sir. Don't you have a daughter
named Katherine, lovely and virtuous?   45

BAPTISTA

I have a daughter, sir, named Katherine.

GREMIO (*to* PETRUCHIO)

You're being too blunt—use a little more tact.

PETRUCHIO

You're wrong, Signor Gremio; let me continue.
(to BAPTISTA) I am a gentleman from Verona, sir,
who, hearing of Katherine's beauty and wit,   50
her pleasant temper and shy modesty,
her wonderful qualities and mild manners,
decided to be so bold as to present myself as an eager guest
at your house, to witness for myself
that which I've so often heard reported.   55
And to pay my admission fee,
I present you with a servant of mine

> HORTENSIO *steps forward.*

who is knowledgeable in music and mathematics.
He'll instruct her well in those sciences
of which I know she's not ignorant.   60
Accept him or you'll hurt my feelings.
His name is Litio, from Mantua.

BAPTISTA

You are welcome, sir, and your servant, too, for your sake.
But as for my daughter, Katherine, I know this—
she won't suit you, much to my regret.   65

PETRUCHIO

I see you don't want the woman to leave home,
or else you don't like me.

BAPTISTA

⨯ Mistake me not; I speak but as I find.
Whence are you, sir? What may I call your name?

PETRUCHIO

70 Petruchio is my name, Antonio's son,
⨯ A man well known throughout all Italy.

BAPTISTA

I know him well; you are welcome for his sake.

GREMIO

Saving your tale, Petruchio, I pray
Let us, that are poor petitioners, speak too.
75 ⨯ *Bacare,** you are marvelous forward.

PETRUCHIO

O, pardon me, Signior Gremio, I would fain be doing.

GREMIO

⨯ I doubt it not, sir; but you will curse your wooing. [*to*
BAPTISTA] Neighbour, this is a gift very grateful, I am sure
of it. To express the like kindness, myself, that have been
80 ⨯ more kindly beholding to you than any, freely give unto
you this young scholar [*presenting* LUCENTIO *disguised as*
⨯ CAMBIO], that hath been long studying at Rheims, as
cunning in Greek, Latin, and other languages, as the other
in music and mathematics. His name is Cambio;* pray
85 accept his service.

BAPTISTA

A thousand thanks, Signior Gremio. Welcome, good
Cambio [*to* TRANIO *as* LUCENTIO]. But, gentle sir,
⨯ methinks you walk like a stranger. May I be so bold to
know the cause of your coming?

TRANIO [*as* LUCENTIO]

90 Pardon me, sir, the boldness is mine own,
⨯ That being a stranger in this city here
Do make myself a suitor to your daughter,
Unto Bianca, fair and virtuous.

---

75 *Bacare* bad Latin for "get back"

84 *Cambio* Italian for "exchange"

BAPTISTA

Don't misunderstand me, sir. I'm telling you the truth.
Where are you from, sir? What is your name?

PETRUCHIO

My name is Petruchio, son of Antonio,   70
a man well-known throughout Italy.

BAPTISTA

I'm very familiar with his name; you're welcome for his sake.

GREMIO

With all due respect to your story, Petruchio, please
let us poor petitioners speak, too.
Back off! You're amazingly eager.   75

PETRUCHIO

Pardon me, Signor Gremio. I just want to get moving.

GREMIO

I don't doubt it, sir, but you'll regret your courting. Neighbor,
Petruchio's gift is very nice, I'm sure. And to express my own
gratitude, I—who am more gratefully indebted to you than
anyone—freely give you this young scholar (LUCENTIO, *as*   80
CAMBIO, *steps forward.*) who has been studying at Rheims for a
long time. He's knowledgeable about Greek, Latin, and other
languages, as well as about music and mathematics. His name
is Cambio. Please accept his service.   85

BAPTISTA

A thousand thanks, Signor Gremio. Welcome, good Cambio.
(*to* TRANIO *as* LUCENTIO) But, sir, I think you look like a stranger
to Padua. May I be so bold as to ask the reason you come here?

TRANIO (*as* LUCENTIO)

Pardon me, sir; I'm the one who should be excused for being   90
    bold,
since, being a stranger here in this city,
I'm making myself a suitor to your daughter,
the lovely and virtuous Bianca.

Nor is your firm resolve unknown to me,
95 In the preferment of the eldest sister.
This liberty is all that I request,
That, upon knowledge of my parentage,
I may have welcome 'mongst the rest that woo,
And free access and favour as the rest;
100 And, toward the education of your daughters,
I here bestow a simple instrument,
And this small packet of Greek and Latin books.

[BIONDELLO *comes forward with the gifts.*]

If you accept them, then their worth is great.

BAPTISTA
Lucentio is your name. Of whence, I pray?

TRANIO [*as* LUCENTIO]
105 Of Pisa, sir, son to Vincentio.

BAPTISTA
A mighty man of Pisa; by report
I know him well. You are very welcome, sir.
[*to* HORTENSIO *as* LITIO] Take you the lute,
[*to* LUCENTIO *as* CAMBIO] and you the set of books.
110 You shall go see your pupils presently.
Holla, within!

Enter a SERVANT.

Sirrah, lead these gentlemen
To my daughters, and tell them both,
These are their tutors. Bid them use them well.

[*Exit* SERVANT, *with* LUCENTIO *and* HORTENSIO,
BIONDELLO *following.*]

115 We will go walk a little in the orchard,
And then to dinner. You are passing welcome,
And so I pray you all to think yourselves.

PETRUCHIO
Signior Baptista, my business asketh haste,
And every day I cannot come to woo.
120 You knew my father well, and in him me,

I know, too, about your firm decision
to see the older sister married first. 95
The only liberty I ask is this:
that once you know who my parents are,
I may be welcome along with the rest of the suitors
and be given the same free access and acceptance as the rest.
And toward the education of your daughters, 100
I give you a simple instrument
and this small package of Greek and Latin books.

> BIONDELLO *steps forward with the lute and books.*

If you accept them, then they're worth a great deal.

BAPTISTA
Your name is Lucentio? Where do you come from?

TRANIO (*as* LUCENTIO)
From Pisa, sir. I'm the son of Vincentio. 105

BAPTISTA
A great man in Pisa; by reputation,
I feel I almost know him. You are most welcome, sir.
(*to* HORTENSIO, *as* LITIO) You take the lute, (*to* LUCENTIO, *as*
    CAMBIO) and you take the set of books.
You'll see your pupils right now. 110
Servant!

> *A* SERVANT *enters.*

Servant, take these gentlemen
to my daughters and tell both of them
that these gentlemen are their tutors. Tell them to treat the
    gentlemen well.

> SERVANT *with* LUCENTIO, HORTENSIO, *and* BIONDELLO
> *following behind all exit.*

We'll go walk a little in the garden 115
and then go to dinner. You are most welcome,
and I hope you'll all think of yourselves that way.

PETRUCHIO
Signor Baptista, my business demands quick action,
and I can't come to court every day.
You knew my father well and through him, me. 120

Left solely heir to all his lands and goods,
X Which I have bettered rather than decreas'd.
Then tell me, if I get your daughter's love,
What dowry shall I have with her to wife?

BAPTISTA

125   After my death the other half of my lands,
And, in possession, twenty thousand crowns.

PETRUCHIO

And, for that dowry, I'll assure her of
Her widowhood, be it that she survive me,
In all my lands and leases whatsoever.

130   X Let specialties be therefore drawn between us,
X That **covenants** may be kept on either hand.

BAPTISTA

Ay, when the special thing is well obtain'd,
That is, her love, for that is all in all.

PETRUCHIO

Why, that is nothing; for I tell you, father,

135   I am as **peremptory** as she proud-minded;
And where two raging fires meet together
They do consume the thing that feeds their fury.
X Though little fire grows great with little wind,
Yet extreme gusts will blow out fire and all. X

140   So I to her, and so she yields to me,
For I am rough and woo not like a babe.

BAPTISTA

Well mayst thou woo, and happy be thy speed!
X But be thou arm'd for some unhappy words.

PETRUCHIO

X Ay, to the proof, as mountains are for winds,

145   X That shake not, though they blow perpetually.

Reenter HORTENSIO [*as* LITIO], *with his head broke.*

BAPTISTA

How now, my friend! Why dost thou look so pale?

I've been left the sole heir to all his land and possessions,
which I've added to, rather than decreased.
So, tell me, if I win your daughter's love,
what dowry will I receive with my wife?

BAPTISTA

After my death, you'll receive half of my lands   125
and when you marry, twenty thousand crowns.

PETRUCHIO

And for that dowry, I'll guarantee her
rights to part of my estate—if she outlives me—
in all my lands and leases.
Let special contracts be drawn up between us   130
so that our vows may be kept by both of us.

BAPTISTA

Certainly; that is after another special thing is obtained—
I mean her love, for that means everything.

PETRUCHIO

Why, that's a mere detail. I tell you, sir,
that I'm as quick to have my way as she is stubborn;   135
and when two raging fires meet,
they consume the thing that feeds their rage.
Though a small fire grows large just by a small wind,
large gusts will totally extinguish a fire.
I'll be just like that wind to her, and so she'll give in to me,   140
for I'm rough and I don't court like a child.

BAPTISTA

Court her well, then, and more luck to you.
But be prepared for some unpleasant words.

PETRUCHIO

I will be shielded against the worst; like mountains are to the
    winds—
the mountains don't shake, though the winds blow all the time.   145

HORTENSIO (*as* LITIO) *enters with his head injured.*

BAPTISTA

What happened, my friend? Why do you look so pale?

HORTENSIO [*as* LITIO]
For fear, I promise you, if I look pale.

BAPTISTA
What, will my daughter prove a good musician?

HORTENSIO [*as* LITIO]
I think she'll sooner prove a soldier.
150 Iron may hold with her, but never lutes.

BAPTISTA
Why, then thou canst not break her to the lute?

HORTENSIO [*as* LITIO]
Why, no, for she hath broke the lute to me.
I did but tell her she mistook her frets,
And bow'd her hand to teach her fingering;
155 When, with a most impatient devilish spirit,
"Frets, call you these?" quoth she. "I'll fume with them!"*
And, with that word, she struck me on the head,
And through the instrument my pate made way;
And there I stood amazed for a while,
160 As on a pillory,* looking through the lute;
While she did call me "rascal fiddler,"
And "twangling Jack," with twenty such vile terms,
As had she studied to misuse me so.

PETRUCHIO
Now, by the world, it is a lusty wench!
165 I love her ten times more than e'er I did.
O, how I long to have some chat with her!

BAPTISTA [*to* HORTENSIO *as* LITIO]
Well, go with me and be not so **discomfited**.
Proceed in practice with my younger daughter.
She's apt to learn and thankful for good turns.—
170 Signior Petruchio, will you go with us,
Or shall I send my daughter Kate to you?

---

156 *fume* Katherine plays with the cliché "fret and fume."

160 *pillory* a wooden collar used on criminals for punishment

HORTENSIO, *as* LITIO
If I look pale, it's out of fear, I swear.

BAPTISTA
Well, will my daughter turn out to be a good musician?

HORTENSIO, *as* LITIO
I think she'll sooner turn out to be a soldier.
Iron may withstand her touch, but never lutes. 150

BAPTISTA
Why, then, can't you break her into playing the lute?

HORTENSIO, *as* LITIO
Why, no—she's broken the lute on my head.
I just told her that she was touching the wrong frets
and bent her hand to teach her the fingering
when, in a very impatient, devilish mood, 155
she said, "Do you call these frets? I'll fume with them."
And with that, she hit me on the head,
and my head pushed clear through the instrument.
There I stood for awhile, stunned,
as if a wooden collar were around my neck, and peered
  through the lute, 160
while she called me a "rascal fiddler,"
a "twanging idiot," and twenty other terrible names
as if she had prepared them beforehand to abuse me.

PETRUCHIO
Well, I declare, that's a lively girl!
I love her ten times more than I did before. 165
Oh, how I long to have a chat with her!

BAPTISTA (*to* HORTENSIO *as* LITIO)
Well, come with me and don't be so downcast.
Continue to teach my younger daughter—
she's willing to learn and grateful for any kindness.—
Signor Petruchio, do you want to go with us, 170
or shall I send my daughter Kate to you?

PETRUCHIO

I pray you do. I will attend her here—

[*Exit all but* PETRUCHIO.]

And woo her with some spirit when she comes.
Say that she rail, why then I'll tell her plain
175   She sings as sweetly as a nightingale.
Say that she frown, I'll say she looks as clear
As morning roses newly wash'd with dew.
Say she be mute and will not speak a word,
Then I'll commend her **volubility**,
180   And say she uttereth piercing **eloquence**.
If she do bid me pack, I'll give her thanks,
As though she bid me stay by her a week.
If she deny to wed, I'll crave the day
When I shall ask the banns* and when be married.
185   But here she comes—and now, Petruchio, speak.

Enter KATHERINE.

Good morrow, Kate, for that's your name, I hear.

KATHERINE

Well have you heard,* but something hard of hearing.
They call me Katherine that do talk of me.

PETRUCHIO

You lie, in faith, for you are call'd plain Kate,*
190   And bonny Kate, and sometimes Kate the curst;
But Kate, the prettiest Kate in Christendom,
Kate of Kate Hall, my super-dainty Kate,
For dainties are all Kates—and therefore, Kate,
Take this of me, Kate of my consolation;
195   Hearing thy mildness praised in every town,
Thy virtues spoke of, and thy beauty sounded,
Yet not so deeply as to thee belongs,
Myself am mov'd to thee for my wife.

---

184   *banns* an announcement of a forthcoming marriage which is made three times
in a church

187   *heard* spoken like "hard" in Elizabethan days

189   *Kate* a play on the word "cates," which are delicate tidbits

PETRUCHIO

Please do that. I'll await her here—

(*Everyone except* PETRUCHIO *exits.*)

and court her with some spirit when she comes.
Suppose she scolds—why then I'll tell her flatly
that she sings as sweetly as a nightingale. 175
Suppose she frowns—I'll say that she looks as cheerful
as morning roses just washed with dew.
Suppose she's silent and refuses to speak a word—
then I'll praise her talkativeness
and say she speaks with keen eloquence. 180
If she tells me to leave, I'll thank her
as if she told me to stay by her side for a week.
If she refuses to marry me, I'll ask her what day
the banns should be spoken and when we should set the
    wedding.
But here she comes—now, Petruchio, speak. 185

KATHERINE *enters.*

Good morning, Kate—for that's your name, I hear.

KATHERINE

You've heard well, but you're a little hard of hearing.
Those who talk about me call me Katherine.

PETRUCHIO

You're lying, you know, for you're called plain Kate,
and fine Kate, and sometimes Kate the shrew. 190
But the prettiest Kate in the Christian world,
Kate of Kate-Hall, my super-dainty Kate—
for dainties are all Kates. So, Kate,
hear me speak, my consoler, Kate:
hearing your mildness praised in every town, 195
your virtues spoken of, and your beauty discussed—
yet not as highly praised as you deserve—
I'm moved to try to persuade you to be my wife.

KATHERINE

"Mov'd!" In good time. Let him that mov'd you hither

200 ✗ Remove you hence. I knew you at the first

✗ You were a moveable.

PETRUCHIO

Why, what's a moveable?

KATHERINE

A joint stool.

PETRUCHIO

Thou hast hit it; come, sit on me.

KATHERINE

205 Asses are made to bear, and so are you.

PETRUCHIO

Women are made to bear, and so are you.

KATHERINE

No such jade as you, if me you mean.

PETRUCHIO

Alas, good Kate, I will not burden thee,

For, knowing thee to be but young and light*—

KATHERINE

210 Too light for such a swain as you to catch,

And yet as heavy as my weight should be.

PETRUCHIO

"Should be"—should buzz!

KATHERINE

Well ta'en, and like a buzzard.

PETRUCHIO

O slow-wing'd turtle, shall a buzzard* take thee?

KATHERINE

215 Ay, for a turtle, as he takes a buzzard.

---

209 *light* means both "spirited" and "loose in morals"

214 *buzzard* Petruchio means a hawk.

KATHERINE
Moved! Well, let the person who moved you here
move you back again. I knew from the beginning   200
that you were a movable.

PETRUCHIO
Why, what's a movable?

KATHERINE
A stool made by a carpenter.

PETRUCHIO
There you have it—come sit on me.

KATHERINE
Asses are made to carry (burdens), and so are you.   205

PETRUCHIO
Women are made to carry (children), and so are you.

KATHERINE
Not an old nag like you, if you're talking about me.

PETRUCHIO
Come, good Kate, I won't burden you
because knowing that you are young and slender—

KATHERINE
Too slender for a rube like you to catch,   210
and yet as heavy as I should be.

PETRUCHIO
Should be! Should—buzz!

KATHERINE
Well-spoken—and just like an idiot.

PETRUCHIO
Oh, you slow-moving turtledove—will a hawk overtake you?

KATHERINE
Yes, he'll mistake me for a turtledove when I'm really a hawk.   215

PETRUCHIO

Come, come, you wasp! I' faith, you are too angry.

KATHERINE

If I be waspish, best beware my sting.

PETRUCHIO

X My remedy is then to pluck it out.

KATHERINE

X Ay, if the fool could find it where it lies.

PETRUCHIO

220   Who knows not where a wasp does wear his sting?
In his tail.

KATHERINE

In his tongue.

PETRUCHIO

X Whose tongue?

KATHERINE

X Yours, if you talk of tales, and so farewell.

PETRUCHIO

225   What, with my tongue in your tail?*
Nay, come again, good Kate. I am a gentleman—

KATHERINE

That I'll try.

      [*She strikes him.*]

PETRUCHIO

I swear I'll cuff you if you strike again.

KATHERINE

So may you lose your arms.
230   X If you strike me, you are no gentleman,
  X And if no gentleman, why then no arms.

---

225   *tongue in your tail* Petruchio turns Katherine's comment into a sexual suggestion.

PETRUCHIO
Come, come, you wasp. Really, you're too angry.

KATHERINE
If I'm waspish, you'd better beware of my sting.

PETRUCHIO
My response then would be to remove your sting.

KATHERINE
Yes, if you could find where it lies, you fool.

PETRUCHIO
Who doesn't know where a wasp keeps its sting?   220
In his tail.

KATHERINE
In his tongue.

PETRUCHIO
Whose tongue?

KATHERINE
Yours, if you tell tales. So, good-bye.

PETRUCHIO
What, with my tongue in your tail?   225
Really, try again.
Good Kate, I'm a gentleman.

KATHERINE
I'll see if that's so.

She hits him.

PETRUCHIO
I swear, I'll hit you if you hit me again.

KATHERINE
Go ahead, if you want to lose your arms.
If you hit me, then you're no gentleman,   230
and if you're no gentleman, why then you don't have a coat of
arms.

PETRUCHIO
A herald, Kate? O, put me in thy books!

KATHERINE
What is your crest?* A coxcomb?*

PETRUCHIO
A combless cock, so Kate will be my hen.

KATHERINE
235   No cock of mine. You crow too like a craven.

PETRUCHIO
Nay, come, Kate, come; you must not look so sour.

KATHERINE
It is my fashion when I see a crab.

PETRUCHIO
Why, here's no crab, and therefore look not sour.

KATHERINE
There is, there is.

PETRUCHIO
240   Then show it me.

KATHERINE
Had I a glass, I would.

PETRUCHIO
What, you mean my face?

KATHERINE
Well aim'd of such a young one.

PETRUCHIO
Now, by Saint George, I am too young for you.

KATHERINE
245   Yet you are wither'd.

---

233   *crest* heraldic symbol

233   *coxcomb* a fool's cap

PETRUCHIO
So you're a scholar of heraldry, Kate? Oh, put me in your heralds' books.

KATHERINE
What's your crest? A coxcomb?

PETRUCHIO
I'll be a tame cock if you'll be my hen, Kate.

KATHERINE
You won't be any cock of mine. You crow too much like a timid rooster.   235

PETRUCHIO
Now come, Kate, come. You must not look so sour.

KATHERINE
I'm like that when I see a crab apple.

PETRUCHIO
Why, there's no crab apple here, so don't look sour.

KATHERINE
Yes, there is.

PETRUCHIO
Then show it to me.   240

KATHERINE
I would if I had a mirror.

PETRUCHIO
What? Do you mean my face?

KATHERINE
That's a nice guess from such a youngster.

PETRUCHIO
By Saint George, I'm too young for you.

KATHERINE
Yet you're wrinkled.   245

PETRUCHIO

'Tis with cares.

KATHERINE

I care not.

PETRUCHIO

Nay, hear you, Kate—in sooth you 'scape not so.

KATHERINE

I chafe you if I tarry. Let me go.

PETRUCHIO

250   No, not a whit. I find you passing gentle.
'Twas told me you were rough and **coy** and sullen.
And now I find report a very liar;
For thou art pleasant, gamesome, passing courteous,
But slow in speech, yet sweet as springtime flowers.
255   Thou canst not frown, thou canst not look askance,
Nor bite the lip as angry wenches will,
Nor hast thou pleasure to be cross in talk.
But thou with mildness entertain'st thy wooers,
With gentle conference, soft and affable.
260   Why does the world report that Kate doth limp?
O sland'rous world! Kate like the hazeltwig
Is straight and slender, and as brown in hue
As hazel nuts, and sweeter than the kernels.
O, let me see thee walk! Thou dost not halt.

KATHERINE

265   Go, fool, and whom thou keep'st command.

PETRUCHIO

Did ever Dian* so become a grove
As Kate this chamber with her princely gait?
O, be thou Dian, and let her be Kate;
And then let Kate be chaste and Dian sportful!

KATHERINE

270   Where did you study all this goodly speech?

PETRUCHIO

It is extempore, from my mother-wit.

---

266   *Dian* or Diana, the Roman goddess of hunting and virginity

PETRUCHIO
That's from worry.

KATHERINE
That's not my worry. (*Starts to leave.*)

PETRUCHIO
Not so fast, Kate. You won't get away so easily.

KATHERINE
I'll harass you if I stay. Let me go.

PETRUCHIO
No, not a bit. I find you very gentle.   250
I heard that you were rough, aloof, and sullen,
and now I see that these reports are lies.
You are pleasant, sporting, very courteous,
perhaps slow to speak, yet sweet as springtime flowers.
You can't even frown; you can't look scornfully   255
or bite your lip as angry women do.
And you don't take pleasure in rough talk.
You receive your suitors with mildness
and gentle conversation, soft and friendly.
Why does everyone say that Kate limps?   260
Oh slanderous world! Kate is like the hazel twig,
straight and slender, and as brown in color
as are hazelnuts, and sweeter than the kernels.
Oh, let me see you walk—why, you don't limp!

KATHERINE
Go, fool, and save those commands for your servants.   265

PETRUCHIO
Did Diana ever set off a grove
as Kate does this chamber with her beautiful walk?
Oh, you be Diana and let Diana be Kate,
and then let Kate be chaste and Diana be sporting.

KATHERINE
Where did you learn all this fine talk?   270

PETRUCHIO
It's all extemporaneous, from my mother wit.

KATHERINE
A witty mother! Witless else her son.

PETRUCHIO
Am I not wise?

KATHERINE
Yes, keep you warm.*

PETRUCHIO

275 Marry, so I mean, sweet Katherine, in thy bed.
And therefore, setting all this chat aside,
Thus in plain terms: your father hath consented
That you shall be my wife, your dowry 'greed on,
And, will you, nill you, I will marry you.

280 Now, Kate, I am a husband for your turn;
For, by this light whereby I see thy beauty,
Thy beauty, that doth make me like thee well,
Thou must be married to no man but me;
For I am he am born to tame you Kate,

285 And bring you from a wild Kate* to a Kate
Conformable as other household Kates.

> *Reenter* BAPTISTA, GREMIO, *and* TRANIO [as
> LUCENTIO].

Here comes your father. Never make denial;
I must and will have Katherine to my wife.

BAPTISTA
Now, Signior Petruchio, how speed you with my daughter?

PETRUCHIO

290 How but well, sir? How but well?
It were impossible I should speed amiss.

BAPTISTA
Why, how now, daughter Katherine? In your dumps?

---

274   *Yes . . . warm.* Kate alludes to a proverb that says even fools have enough
intelligence to keep themselves warm.

285   *wild Kate* a play on the word "wildcat"

KATHERINE

She kept her wit, and left none to her son.

PETRUCHIO

I'm not wise?

KATHERINE

Yes, wise enough to keep yourself warm.

PETRUCHIO

Really, that's just what I mean to do, sweet Katherine—in your   275
bed.
So, putting all this chatting aside,
I'll tell you this in plain language: Your father has agreed
that you will be my wife, your dowry is settled,
and whether you want to or not, I'm going to marry you.
Now, Kate, I'm just the husband to suit you   280
because, by this light that reveals your beauty—
beauty that makes me like you very much—
you must be married to no man except me.
Because I'm the man born to tame you, Kate,
and change you from a wild Kate to a Kate   285
as agreeable as any other housewife Kate.

> BAPTISTA, GREMIO, *and* TRANIO (*as* LUCENTIO) *enter.*

Here comes your father. Don't try to fight it—
I must and will have you to be my wife.

BAPTISTA

Now, Signor Petruchio, how are you getting on with my
daughter?

PETRUCHIO

How else but well, sir? How else but well?   290
It would be impossible that I should not get along well with her.

BAPTISTA

What's wrong, daughter Katherine? Are you sulking?

KATHERINE

    Call you me daughter? Now I promise you
    You have show'd a tender fatherly regard,
295   To wish me wed to one half lunatic,
    A mad-cap ruffian and a swearing Jack,
    That thinks with oaths to face the matter out.

PETRUCHIO

    Father, 'tis thus: yourself and all the world,
    That talk'd of her, have talk'd amiss of her.
300   If she be curst, it is for policy,
    For she's not froward, but modest as the dove;
    She is not hot, but **temperate** as the morn;
    For patience she will prove a second Grissel,*
    And Roman Lucrece* for her chastity;
305   And to conclude, we have 'greed so well together
    That upon Sunday is the wedding day.

KATHERINE

    I'll see thee hang'd on Sunday first.

GREMIO

    Hark, Petruchio, she says she'll see thee hang'd first.

TRANIO [*as* LUCENTIO]

    Is this your speeding? Nay, then, good night our part!

PETRUCHIO

310   Be patient, gentlemen. I choose her for myself.
    If she and I be pleas'd, what's that to you?
    'Tis bargain'd 'twixt us twain, being alone,
    That she shall still be curst in company.
    I tell you, 'tis incredible to believe
315   How much she loves me. O, the kindest Kate!
    She hung about my neck, and kiss on kiss
    She vied so fast, protesting oath on oath,
    That in a twink she won me to her love.
    O, you are novices! 'Tis a world to see

---

303   *Grissel* the patient wife in Boccaccio's *Decameron* and in Chaucer's "Clerk's Tale"

304   *Lucrece* Roman woman who killed herself after she was raped. Shakespeare wrote a poem, *The Rape of Lucrece*, about her.

KATHERINE

You call me your daughter? Well, I swear,
you have shown me tender, fatherly respect
to wish me to marry a man who's half a lunatic,   295
a crazy rascal, and a swearing scoundrel,
who thinks he can bluff his way through anything with oaths.

PETRUCHIO

Sir, it's like this: You and everyone else
that have spoken of her have mistaken what she's like.
If she is shrewish, that's just a front   300
because she's not willful but modest as the dove.
She is not hot-tempered but as cool as the morning.
As for patience, she will turn out to be another Grissel
and like the Roman Lucrece for her chastity.
So, to conclude, we're in such agreement with one another   305
that we've set the wedding for next Sunday.

KATHERINE

I'll see you hanged on Sunday first.

GREMIO

Listen, Petruchio, she said she'd see you hanged first.

TRANIO (*as* LUCENTIO)

Is this the headway you've made? Well, then, farewell to
our suits!

PETRUCHIO

Be patient, gentlemen. I'm choosing her for myself.   310
If she and I are satisfied, what difference does that make to you?
We settled between us when we were alone
that she should always be shrewish when other people are
around.
I tell you, it's hard to believe
how much she loves me. Oh, kindest Kate!   315
She put her arms around my neck and kissed
me faster and faster, swearing she loved me again and again,
so that in a twinkling, she'd made me fall in love with her.
Oh, you are novices! It's a wonder to see

320 How tame, when men and women are alone,
A meacock wretch can make the curstest shrew.—
Give me thy hand, Kate. I will unto Venice
To buy apparel 'gainst the wedding day.—
Provide the feast, father, and bid the guests;
325 I will be sure my Katherine shall be fine.

BAPTISTA
I know not what to say, but give me your hands.
God send you joy, Petruchio! 'Tis a match.

GREMIO / TRANIO [*as* LUCENTIO]
Amen, say we. We will be witnesses.

PETRUCHIO
Father, and wife, and gentlemen, adieu.
330 I will to Venice; Sunday comes apace.
We will have rings and things and fine array;
And kiss me, Kate. We will be married o' Sunday.

[*Exit* PETRUCHIO *and* KATHERINE *through different doors.*]

GREMIO
Was ever match clapp'd up so suddenly?

BAPTISTA
Faith, gentlemen, now I play a merchant's part,
335 And venture madly on a desperate mart.

TRANIO [*as* LUCENTIO]
'Twas a commodity lay fretting* by you.
'Twill bring you gain, or perish on the seas.

BAPTISTA
The gain I seek, is quiet in the match.

GREMIO
No doubt but he hath got a quiet catch.
340 But now, Baptista, to your younger daughter.
Now is the day we long have looked for.
I am your neighbour and was suitor first.

---

336 *fretting* means both "bothering" and "rotting away"

when men and women are alone how tame 320
a timid wretch can make the shrillest shrew.
Give me your hand, Kate. I'll go to Venice
to buy clothes for our wedding.
You set up the feast, father-in-law, and invite the guests.
I want to be sure my Katherine will look fine. 325

BAPTISTA
I don't know what to say. Well, give me your hands.
God bring you joy, Petruchio, you and Katherine will be
married.

GREMIO and **TRANIO**, *as* LUCENTIO
We say amen to that; we'll be witnesses.

PETRUCHIO
Father and wife and gentlemen: good-bye.
I'm off for Venice. Sunday isn't far off. 330
We must have rings and things and fine clothing.
Kiss me, Kate; we'll be married on Sunday.

> PETRUCHIO *and* KATHERINE *exit.*

GREMIO
Was there ever a match made so quickly?

BAPTISTA
In truth, gentlemen, now I play the part of a merchant
and gamble like a madman on a risky deal. 335

TRANIO, *as* LUCENTIO
You're dealing in a commodity that was rotting away in the
warehouse.
It will bring you a profit or else be lost at sea.

BAPTISTA
The profit I'm looking for in the marriage is quiet.

GREMIO
There's no doubt but that he has caught a quiet catch.
But now, Baptista, about your younger daughter: 340
this is the day we've long been waiting for.
I'm your neighbor, and I was the first suitor.

TRANIO [*as* LUCENTIO]
And I am one that love Bianca more
Than words can witness or your thoughts can guess.

GREMIO

345 Youngling, thou canst not love so dear as I.

TRANIO [*as* LUCENTIO]
Greybeard, thy love doth freeze.

GREMIO

But thine doth fry.
Skipper, stand back! 'Tis age that nourisheth.

TRANIO [*as* LUCENTIO]
But youth in ladies' eyes that flourisheth.

BAPTISTA

350 Content you, gentlemen; I will compound this strife.
'Tis deeds must win the prize, and he of both
That can assure my daughter greatest dower
Shall have my Bianca's love.
Say, Signior Gremio, what can you assure her?

GREMIO

355 First, as you know, my house within the city
Is richly furnished with plate and gold,
Basin and ewers to lave her dainty hands;
My hangings all of Tyrian tapestry;
In ivory coffers I have stuff'd my crowns,
360 In cypress chests my arras counterpoints,
Costly apparel, tents, and canopies,
Fine linen, Turkey cushions boss'd with pearl,
Valance of Venice gold in needlework,
Pewter and brass and all things that belongs
365 To house or housekeeping. Then, at my farm
I have a hundred milch-kine to the pail,
Six score fat oxen standing in my stalls,
And all things answerable to this portion.
Myself am struck in years, I must confess,
370 And if I die tomorrow, this is hers,
If whilst I live she will be only mine.

TRANIO, *as* LUCENTIO
 And I'm the one that loves Bianca more
 than words can express or thoughts can guess.

GREMIO
 Youngster, you can't love her as much as I do. 345

TRANIO, *as* LUCENTIO
 Old man, your love is cold.

GREMIO
 But yours is too hot.
 Stand back, whippersnapper! It's age that brings prosperity.

TRANIO, *as* LUCENTIO
 But it's youth that's most highly valued by ladies.

BAPTISTA
 Stop fighting, gentlemen; I'll settle this argument. 350
 It's deeds that will win the prize, and whichever one of you
 can guarantee my daughter the largest wedding gift
 will have Bianca's love.
 So, tell me, Signor Gremio, what can you promise her?

GREMIO
 First, as you know, my house in the city 355
 is filled with silverware and gold.
 I have basins and pitchers to wash her dainty hands.
 My hangings are all purple tapestries;
 I've stuffed my money in ivory coffers.
 In my cypress chests, I have my French tapestries, 360
 expensive clothing, bedspreads, and canopies.
 I have delicate linens, Turkish cushions embroidered with pearl,
 bed drapes from Venice done in gold stitchery,
 pewter, and brass, and everything that
 a house or housekeeper should have. Then, at my farm, 365
 I have a hundred cows who give milk that I sell,
 one hundred twenty fat oxen standing in their stalls,
 and everything else fitting the scale of operations I just
  described.
 I must confess that I'm old.
 So if I die tomorrow, all of this is hers. 370
 And while I live, she will be my only concern and heir.

TRANIO [*as* LUCENTIO]

That "only" came well in. [*to* BAPTISTA] Sir, list to me.
I am my father's heir and only son.
If I may have your daughter to my wife,
I'll leave her houses three or four as good,
Within rich Pisa walls, as any one
Old Signior Gremio has in Padua,
Besides|two thousand ducats* by the year
Of fruitful land, all which shall be her jointure.—
What, have I pinch'd you, Signior Gremio?

GREMIO

Two thousand ducats by the year of land!
[*aside*] My land amounts not to so much in all.—
That she shall have, besides an argosy
That now is lying in Marcellus's road.
[*to* TRANIO] What, have I chok'd you with an argosy?

TRANIO [*as* LUCENTIO]

Gremio, 'tis known my father hath no less
Than three great argosies, besides two galliasses
And twelve tight galleys. These I will assure her,
And twice as much, whate'er thou off'rest next.

GREMIO

Nay, I have off'red all, I have no more;
And she can have no more than all I have.
[*to* BAPTISTA] If you like me, she shall have me and mine.

TRANIO [*as* LUCENTIO]

Why, then the maid is mine from all the world,
By your firm promise; Gremio is outvied.

BAPTISTA

I must confess your offer is the best;
And, let your father make her the assurance,
She is your own; else, you must pardon me,
If you should die before him, where's her dower?

TRANIO [*as* LUCENTIO]

That's but a **cavil**. He is old, I young.

---

378   *ducats* gold coins

TRANIO, *as* LUCENTIO
    That "only" is well to the point. (*to* BAPTISTA) Sir, listen to me:
    I am my father's heir and his only son.
    If your daughter marries me,
    I'll leave her three or four houses   375
    in rich Pisa as good as any that
    old Signor Gremio has in Padua.
    Besides that, I'll give her two thousand ducats every year
    from fertile land—all of that will be her settlement.
    Well, are you feeling the heat, Signor Gremio?   380

GREMIO
    Two thousand ducats a year from your land!
    (*aside*) The price of my land doesn't even total that much!
    (*to* BAPTISTA) Well, she'll get that, besides a merchant ship
    that's now docked at Marseilles' harbor.
    (*to* TRANIO) So, have I choked you with the ship?   385

TRANIO, *as* LUCENTIO
    Gremio, it's well known that my father has no less
    than three big ships, besides two large galleys
    and twelve well-built galleys. I'll guarantee her those
    and twice as much as whatever you offer next.

GREMIO
    No, I've offered everything—I don't have anything more,   390
    and she can't have more than everything I have.
    (*to* BAPTISTA) If you prefer me, she will have me and all I own.

TRANIO, *as* LUCENTIO
    Then the girl is mine and no one else's
    according to your firm promise. I've outbid Gremio.

BAPTISTA
    I must confess, your offer is the best.   395
    If you have your father guarantee her the settlement,
    then she's yours. Otherwise you'll excuse me for saying so,
    where is her settlement if you should die before your father?

TRANIO, *as* LUCENTIO
    That's just a detail. He is old; I'm young.

GREMIO

400 X And may not young men die, as well as old?

BAPTISTA

Well, gentlemen, I am thus resolv'd:

X On Sunday next you know

X My daughter Katherine is to be married.

[*to* TRANIO *as* LUCENTIO] Now, on the Sunday

405   following, shall Bianca

Be bride to you, if you make this assurance.

If not, to Signior Gremio.

And so, I take my leave, and thank you both.

GREMIO

Adieu, good neighbour. [*Exit* BAPTISTA.]

410   Now I fear thee not.

Sirrah young gamester, your father were a fool

X   To give thee all, and in his **waning** age

Set foot under thy table. Tut, a toy!

An old Italian fox is not so kind, my boy.

[*Exit.*]

TRANIO

415 X A vengeance on your crafty withered hide!—

X Yet I have fac'd it with a card of ten.

X 'Tis in my head to do my master good.

I see no reason but suppos'd Lucentio

Must get* a father, call'd "suppos'd Vincentio"—

420 X And that's a wonder. Fathers commonly

X Do get their children; but in this case of wooing,

A child shall get a sire, if I fail not of my cunning.

[*Exit.*]

---

419 *get* Tranio makes a pun on the double meaning of get: "to find" and "to father,"
or "beget."

GREMIO

And can't young men die just as quickly as old men? 400

BAPTISTA

Well, gentlemen,
I've decided this. You know that on next Sunday,
my daughter Katherine is to be married.
(*to* TRANIO, *as* LUCENTIO) Now, on the following Sunday, Bianca will
marry you if you make that guarantee. 405
If not, she'll marry Signor Gremio.
And with that, I'll leave and thank both of you.

GREMIO

Good-bye, good neighbor. (BAPTISTA *exits.*) Now I'm not afraid
of you.
Foolish young gambler, your father would have to be a fool 410
to give you everything in his old age
and become your dependent. Nonsense, what rubbish!
An old Italian fox is not so generous my boy.

Exit.

TRANIO

Damn your crafty, wrinkled hide! 415
Still, I've bluffed with a low card.
I think I know how to help my master.
I see no other way out except to get "Lucentio"
a father, who will be called the "sham Vincentio."
And that's amazing—fathers generally 420
sire their own children. But in this case of courting,
a child will produce a father, if my cunning doesn't fail me.

Exit.

Act II Review

Discussion Questions

1. Why does Kate abuse Bianca?

2. How does Petruchio's first meeting with Baptista set the style for the rest of the courtship?

3. What kind of father does Baptista appear to be?

4. What purpose is served by Hortensio/Litio's account of his music lesson with Kate?

5. Does Petruchio's soliloquy reveal a concealed character?

6. Why are puns used so frequently in Kate and Petruchio's encounter?

7. Why is Petruchio's story about Kate's agreement to marry him so readily accepted?

8. How does Tranio's decision to find a "father" reflect a theme of the play?

Literary Elements

1. A **pun** is a humorous play on words. Kate and Petruchio's encounter in Act II is rich in this kind of wordplay. Find as many puns as you can, and explain their double meanings. What do you think is the purpose of this kind of exchange?

2. A comparison between two unlike things using *like* or *as* is a **simile**. Note any similes you find in Act II. How do you think they contribute to the play?

3. In drama, a **foil** is a character who provides strong contrast to another character. In what ways is Bianca a foil to her older sister Kate?

4. **Irony** is the opposite of what might be expected. Given what you know about Kate, what examples of irony can you find in Petruchio's words in Act II?

Writing Prompts

1. Summarize the action of the play so far. Use one sentence for Act I and one for Act II.

2. Choose a quotation from one of the scenes in Act I or Act II that you feel best characterizes that scene. In a paragraph, discuss why you think this quotation is significant and effective at conveying the events or emotions of this scene.

3. Imagine you have just been cast in a play and one of your fellow actors is playing Petruchio. Describe the actor in an email to your friend, and say whether you think he is well cast.

4. Some people have trouble telling all of Bianca's suitors (Gremio, Lucentio, and Hortensio) apart. Pretend you are a casting director. Cast current actors in these four roles, striving for contrast. Write a paragraph that explains the reasons for your decisions.

5. Rewrite Petruchio's "plain Kate, bonny Kate" speech in Act II in which he makes clear he means to marry her. Using the name of your choice and different details, write a proposal of marriage with a similar satiric tone.

The Taming of the Shrew

ACT III

Richard Burton and Elizabeth Taylor in Zeffirelli film, 1967

"Such a mad marriage never was before."

Before You Read

1. At this point in the play, which character strikes you as more vivid and compelling, Petruchio or Kate? Explain why.

3. Describe what kind of wedding you might expect Kate and Petruchio to have. Then compare your version with their actual wedding in Act III.

4. Look for hints in Act III that Bianca has a mind of her own.

Literary Elements

1. Characters in *The Taming of the Shrew* often cite long lists of **descriptive details** that paint a vivid word picture for the audience. In Act II, Scene i, Bianca's suitor Gremio tries to impress Baptista with his wealth by listing his possessions, from "ivory coffers" stuffed with crowns to "six score fat oxen."

2. **Farce** is a type of exaggerated comedy, full of coincidence and ridiculous events. **Slapstick** refers to low physical comedy, including pratfalls, face-slapping, and other rude and noisy gestures. *The Taming of the Shrew* employs farce and slapstick in Act II when Kate abuses her music teacher, Hortensio/Litio, with a lute over his head.

3. An **epithet** is a word or phrase used to characterize someone, as when Kate is referred to as a "shrew"—someone who is mean and bossy. It is often a form of contempt or name-calling. At the beginning of Act III, Hortensio/Litio calls Lucentio/Cambio a "wrangling pedant," meaning a quarrelsome, finicky teacher.

4. A **symbol** is a person, object, action, or place that stands for something beyond its obvious meaning. When Petruchio first meets Katherina and immediately nicknames her "Kate," it is symbolic; he is putting her in her place by using the diminutive form of her name.

Words to Know

The following vocabulary words appear in Act III in the original text of Shakespeare's play. However, they are words that are still used today. Read the definitions here, and pay attention to the words as you read the play (they will be in boldfaced type).

clamorous	noisy; loud
construe [conster]	understand; take to mean
digress	ramble; stray
gamut	range; scope
pithy	concise; to the point
plead	beg; appeal
preposterous	absurd; outrageous
prerogative	privilege; right
rudiments	basics; fundamentals
suffice [sufficeth]	be enough or sufficient

Left to right: Hortensio, Lucentio, Bianca, Royal Shakespeare Company, 1995

Act Summary

Undercover as tutors, Lucentio and Hortensio vie for Bianca's love. While giving Bianca a Latin lesson, Lucentio lets her in on his true identity. She is cagey but gives him reason to hope. Hortensio delivers a love note to her during their music lesson, but his efforts are not received so well. He decides that Bianca's interest in the "lowly" Lucentio is a mark against her good taste. If she persists, he will no longer woo her.

On Sunday, Petruchio shows up late at his wedding to Kate, dressed like a madman. During the delay, Tranio tells his master Lucentio of his plans for finding a replacement for Vincentio, Lucentio's real father. Baptista wants to meet Vincentio in order to discuss the terms of Bianca's dowry.

After the wedding is over, an outraged Gremio relays to Tranio the behavior of Petruchio and Kate at their wedding. Petruchio swore and cuffed the priest and gave Kate a lip-smacking kiss that echoed throughout the church.

To further provoke his new wife, Petruchio refuses to allow her to attend her own wedding feast. Defiant, but unable to resist, Kate is carted off to Petruchio's country home.

ACT III, SCENE I

[*Padua. Baptista's house.*] *Enter* LUCENTIO,
HORTENSIO, *and* BIANCA.

LUCENTIO [*as* CAMBIO]
Fiddler, forbear; you grow too forward, sir.
Have you so soon forgot the entertainment
Her sister Katherine welcom'd you withal?

HORTENSIO [*as* LITIO]
But, wrangling pedant, this is
5   The patroness of heavenly harmony.
Then give me leave to have **prerogative**;
And when in music we have spent an hour,
Your lecture shall have leisure for as much.

LUCENTIO [*as* CAMBIO]
Preposterous* ass, that never read so far
10   To know the cause why music was ordain'd!
Was it not to refresh the mind of man
After his studies or his usual pain?
Then give me leave to read philosophy,
And, while I pause, serve in your harmony.

HORTENSIO [*as* LITIO]
15   Sirrah, I will not bear these braves of thine.

BIANCA
Why, gentlemen, you do me double wrong
To strive for that which resteth in my choice.
I am no breeching scholar in the schools.
I'll not be tied to hours nor 'pointed times,
20   But learn my lessons as I please myself.
And, to cut off all strife, here sit we down;
[*to* HORTENSIO] Take you your instrument, play you the
      whiles;
His lecture will be done ere you have tun'd.

HORTENSIO [*as* LITIO]
25   You'll leave his lecture when I am in tune?

---

9   *preposterous* in Shakespeare's times, meant putting secondary things first. The
Greek philosopher Aristotle said study should come before music.

ACT 3, SCENE 1

Padua. BAPTISTA'S *house.* LUCENTIO, HORTENSIO, *and* BIANCA *enter.*

LUCENTIO, *as* CAMBIO
Fiddler, ease off; you're getting too eager, sir.
Have you so quickly forgotten the welcome reception
given you by Katherine?

HORTENSIO, *as* LITIO
But, you quarrelsome know-it-all, this is
the patroness of heavenly harmony. 5
So let me go first,
and after we've spent an hour with music,
you can give just as much time for your lesson.

LUCENTIO, *as* CAMBIO
You backward fool, you're not even well-read enough
to know the reason why music was created! 10
Wasn't the reason to refresh man's mind
after studying or usual work?
Therefore, let me lecture in philosophy,
and whenever I stop, present your tunes.

HORTENSIO, *as* LITIO
Servant, I won't stand for these impudent speeches of yours. 15

BIANCA
Why, gentlemen, you both do me wrong
by trying to decide that which is up to me.
I'm no schoolgirl ready for the teacher's whip.
I won't be tied to a schedule or appointments;
I'll learn my lessons when it suits me. 20
So, to end the argument, we'll sit down here.
(*to* HORTENSIO) You, take your instrument and play in the
     meanwhile.
His lesson will be finished before you've even tuned up.

HORTENSIO, *as* LITIO
You'll stop studying his lesson when I have tuned up? 25

LUCENTIO [*as* CAMBIO]

That will be never. [*to* HORTENSIO] Tune your instrument.

BIANCA

Where left we last?

LUCENTIO [*as* CAMBIO]

Here, madam:

    Hic ibat Simois; hic est Sigeia tellus;

30   *Hic steterat Priami regia celsa senis.* *

BIANCA

Conster* them.

LUCENTIO [*as* CAMBIO]

Hic ibat, as I told you before, *Simois,* I am Lucentio,
hic est, son unto Vincentio of Pisa, *Sigeia tellus,*
disguised thus to get your love; *Hic steterat,* and that
35   Lucentio that comes a-wooing, *Priami,* is my man
Tranio, *regia,* bearing my port, *celsa senis,* that we
might beguile the old pantaloon.

HORTENSIO [*as* LITIO]

Madam, my instrument's in tune.

BIANCA

Let's hear. [*He plays.*] O fie! the treble jars.

LUCENTIO [*as* CAMBIO]

40   Spit in the hole, man, and tune again.

BIANCA

Now let me see if I can conster it:
Hic ibat Simois, I know you not; *hic est Sigeia tellus,* I
trust you not; *Hic steterat Priami,* take heed he hear us
not; *regia,* presume not; *celsa senis,* despair not.

HORTENSIO [*as* LITIO]

45   Madam, 'tis now in tune. [*He plays again.*]

LUCENTIO [*as* CAMBIO]

                All but the bass.

29–30   *Hic . . . senis*   a quote from the Roman poet Ovid's *Heriodes.* "Here flowed the
Simois; here is the Sigeian land; / Here had stood old Priam's high palace."
Sigeia was the site of many battles in the Trojan War.

31   *Conster* construe or interpret

LUCENTIO, *as* CAMBIO

That will never happen; go tune your instrument.

BIANCA

Where did we stop last time?

LUCENTIO, *as* CAMBIO

Here, madam:

"Here flowed the Simois; here is the Sigeian land;

Here stood ancient Priam's high palace." 30

BIANCA

Translate that.

LUCENTIO, *as* CAMBIO

Hic ibat means as I told you before. *Simois*, I am Lucentio. *Hic
est*, son of Vincentio of Pisa. *Sigeia tellus*, disguised like this to
win your love. *Hic steterat*, and the Lucentio who is courting 35
you, *Priami*, is my servant Tranio, *regia*, acting my part, *celsa
senis*, that we might trick the old pantaloon.

HORTENSIO, *as* LITIO

Madam, my instrument is in tune.

BIANCA

Let's hear. Oh, heavens, the treble note is jarring!

LUCENTIO, *as* CAMBIO

Give it another try, man, and tune it again. 40

BIANCA

Now let me see if I can translate it.

Hic ibat Simois, I don't know you. *Hic est Sigeia tellus*, I don't
trust you. *Hic steterat Priami*, be careful he doesn't overhear us.
Regia, don't overstep your boundaries. *Celsa senis*, don't despair.

HORTENSIO, *as* LITIO

Madam, it's tuned up now. (*He plays again.*) 45

LUCENTIO, *as* CAMBIO

Everything but the bass notes.

HORTENSIO [*as* LITIO]
　　The bass is right; 'tis the base knave that jars.
　　[*aside*] How fiery and forward our pedant is.
　　Now, for my life, the knave doth court my love!
50　Pedascule,* I'll watch you better yet.

BIANCA [*to* LUCENTIO]
　　In time I may believe, yet I mistrust.

LUCENTIO [*as* CAMBIO]
　　Mistrust it not; for, sure, Aeacides*
　　Was Ajax, call'd so from his grandfather.

BIANCA
　　I must believe my master; else, I promise you,
55　I should be arguing still upon that doubt.
　　But let it rest.—Now, Litio, to you.
　　Good master, take it not unkindly, pray,
　　That I have been thus pleasant with you both.

HORTENSIO [*as* LITIO *to* LUCENTIO]
　　You may go walk, and give me leave awhile.
60　My lessons make no music in three parts.

LUCENTIO [*as* CAMBIO]
　　Are you so formal, sir? Well, I must wait,
　　[*aside*] And watch withal, for, but I be deceiv'd,
　　Our fine musician groweth amorous.

HORTENSIO [*as* LITIO]
　　Madam, before you touch the instrument,
65　To learn the order of my fingering,
　　I must begin with **rudiments** of art,
　　To teach you **gamut** in a briefer sort,
　　More pleasant, **pithy**, and effectual,
　　Than hath been taught by any of my trade.
70　And there it is in writing fairly drawn.

BIANCA
　　Why, I am past my gamut long ago.

50　*Pedascule* bad Latin for "little pedant"

52　*Aeacides* Ajax, a Greek warrior who fought against the Trojans. Here Lucentio pretends to interpret the Roman poet Ovid to Bianca.

HORTENSIO, *as* LITIO
The low notes are in tune, it's just the low rascal that's jarring.
(*aside*) How hot-blooded and eager our pedant is!
I'd swear on my life that the rascal is courting my love.
Little pedant, I'll keep a closer watch on you than before.   50

BIANCA (*to* LUCENTIO)
In time I may believe you, yet now I have doubts.

LUCENTIO (*as* CAMBIO)
Don't doubt me, Aeacides
was definitely called Ajax—named that for his grandfather.

BIANCA
I must believe my teacher. Otherwise, I swear to you
that I would still argue the question.   55
But let it go. (*to* HORTENSIO) Now, Litio, I'll learn from you.
Good teacher, please don't be offended, I beg you,
that I've been so lighthearted with both of you.

HORTENSIO, *as* LITIO (*to* LUCENTIO)
You can take a walk and leave me alone for a bit.
My lessons don't have music for three voices.   60

LUCENTIO, *as* CAMBIO
You want to be so formal, sir? (*aside*) Well, I must wait
and watch, too, because unless I'm deceived,
our fine musician is falling in love.

HORTENSIO, *as* LITIO
Madam, before you touch the instrument
to learn where to put your fingers,   65
I must begin with the basics of the art
to teach you a scale of a shorter kind,
more pleasant, succinct, and effective
than has been taught by any of my fellow music teachers.
And there it is in writing, nicely written.   70

BIANCA
Why, I learned the scales a long time ago.

HORTENSIO [*as* LITIO]
Yet read the gamut of Hortensio. [*giving her a paper*]

BIANCA [*Reads.*]
"*Gamut* I am, the ground of all accord,
A re, to **plead** Hortensio's passions.
75   *B mi*, Bianca, take him for thy lord,
C fa ut, that loves with all affection.
D sol re, one clef, two notes have I.
E la mi, show pity, or I die."
Call you this "gamut"? Tut, I like it not.
80   Old fashions please me best; I am not so nice
To change true rules for odd inventions.

            Enter a MESSENGER.

MESSENGER
Mistress, your father prays you leave your books
And help to dress your sister's chamber up.
You know tomorrow is the wedding day.

BIANCA
85   Farewell, sweet masters both; I must be gone.

            [*Exit* BIANCA *and* MESSENGER.]

LUCENTIO
Faith, mistress, then I have no cause to stay.

            [*Exit.*]

HORTENSIO
But I have cause to pry into this pedant.
Methinks he looks as though he were in love.
Yet if thy thoughts, Bianca, be so humble
90   To cast thy wand'ring eyes on every stale,
Seize thee that list! If once I find thee ranging,
Hortensio will be quit with thee by changing.

            [*Exit.*]

HORTENSIO, *as* LITIO
Still, read Hortensio's scale. (*Gives her a paper.*)

BIANCA (*Reads.*)
"*Gamut*, I am the scale, the beginning of all harmony.
A re, to urge Hortensio's passion;
B mi, Bianca, take him as your husband;   75
C fa ut, who loves you with all his heart;
D sol re, I have one clef and two notes;
E la mi, show me mercy or I'll die."
Do you call this a scale? Nonsense, I don't like it.
Old-fashioned things please me the best. I'm not so whimsical   80
as to change true rules for strange inventions.

   A MESSENGER *enters.*

MESSENGER
Mistress, your father asks you to leave your books
and help decorate your sister's room.
You know tomorrow is her wedding day.

BIANCA
Good-bye, both of you sweet teachers. I must go.   85

   BIANCA *and* MESSENGER *exit.*

LUCENTIO
Well then, mistress, I have no reason to stay.

   Exit.

HORTENSIO
But I have reason to investigate this know-it-all.
I thought he looked as though he were in love.
Yet if your affections, Bianca, can stoop so low
so that you cast your wandering eye on every decoy,   90
let whoever wants you have you. If I once find you straying,
I'll leave you by changing lovers.

   Exit.

ACT III, SCENE II

[*Padua. Before Baptista's house.*] *Enter*, BAPTISTA, GREMIO, TRANIO [*as* LUCENTIO], KATHERINE, BIANCA, LUCENTIO [*as* CAMBIO], *and others*, ATTENDANTS.

BAPTISTA [*to* TRANIO]
Signior Lucentio, this is the 'pointed day
That Katherine and Petruchio should be married,
And yet we hear not of our son-in-law.
What will be said? What mockery will it be,
5   To want the bridegroom when the priest attends
To speak the ceremonial rites of marriage!
What says Lucentio to this shame of ours?

KATHERINE
No shame but mine. I must, forsooth, be forc'd
To give my hand oppos'd against my heart,
10   Unto a mad-brain rudesby full of spleen,
Who woo'd in haste and means to wed at leisure.
I told you, I, he was a frantic fool,
Hiding his bitter jests in blunt behaviour,
And, to be noted for a merry man,
15   He'll woo a thousand, 'point the day of marriage,
Make friends, invite, and proclaim the banns,
Yet never means to wed where he hath woo'd.
Now must the world point at poor Katherine,
And say, "Lo, there is mad Petruchio's wife,
20   If it would please him come and marry her!"

TRANIO [*as* LUCENTIO]
Patience, good Katherine, and Baptista too.
Upon my life, Petruchio means but well,
Whatever fortune stays him from his word.
Though he be blunt, I know him passing wise;
25   Though he be merry, yet withal he's honest.

KATHERINE
Would Katherine had never seen him, though!

She exits weeping.

ACT 3, SCENE 2

Padua. Before BAPTISTA's house. BAPTISTA, GREMIO, TRANIO (*as* LUCENTIO), KATHERINE, BIANCA, LUCENTIO (*as* CAMBIO), *and other guests, as well as* SERVANTS, *all enter.*

BAPTISTA (*to* TRANIO)
Signor Lucentio, this is the scheduled day
for Katherine and Petruchio to be married,
and yet I haven't heard from my son-in-law.
What will people say? What a cruel joke it will be
if the bridegroom is missing when the priest appears   5
to say the ceremonial wedding ritual!
What do you say, Lucentio, about this embarrassment?

KATHERINE
No one has been embarrassed except me. Really, I'm to be
    forced
to marry against my will
a crazy, rude fellow, full of insane impulses,   10
who courted with such speed, and means to be married in his
    own good time.
I told you that he was a mad fool,
hiding his bitter jokes in crude behavior.
And to be known as a jolly fellow,
he'll court a thousand women, set the marriage date,   15
provide the feast, invite guests, and have the banns read—
yet he never intends to marry the one he's courted.
Now everyone in the world will point at poor Katherine
and say, "Look! There's crazy Petruchio's wife—
if he wanted to come and marry her."   20

TRANIO, *as* LUCENTIO
Be patient, good Katherine and you, too, Baptista.
I swear on my life that Petruchio has only good intentions,
whatever might be holding him from keeping his word.
He might be rough, but I know he's sensible.
He might be a joker, yet, nevertheless, he's truthful.   25

KATHERINE
Yet, I wish that I had never seen him!

Exits weeping, followed by BIANCA *and others.*

BAPTISTA

Go, girl. I cannot blame thee now to weep,
For such an injury would vex a very saint,
Much more a shrew of thy impatient humour.

Enter BIONDELLO.

BIONDELLO

30 Master, master! News! And such old news as you never
heard of!

BAPTISTA

Is it new and old too? How may that be?

BIONDELLO

Why, is it not news to hear of Petruchio's coming?

BAPTISTA

Is he come?

BIONDELLO

35 Why, no, sir.

BAPTISTA

What then?

BIONDELLO

He is coming.

BAPTISTA

When will he be here?

BIONDELLO

When he stands where I am and sees you there.

TRANIO [*as* LUCENTIO]

40 But say, what to thine old news?

BIONDELLO

Why, Petruchio is coming in a new hat and an old jerkin;
a pair of old breeches thrice turn'd;* a pair of boots that
have been candle-cases, one buckled, another lac'd; an old
rusty sword ta'en out of the town armoury, with a broken
45 hilt, and chapeless; with two broken points;* his horse
hipp'd with an old mothy saddle and stirrups of no

---

42 *thrice turned* turned inside out three times to hide signs of wear

45 *points* laces that tied a man's hose to his breeches

BAPTISTA

Depart, girl! I can't blame you for crying now,
for an insult like you've received would irritate even a saint,
much less a shrew with your impatient temper.

BIONDELLO *enters.*

BIONDELLO

Master, master! News! Old news and news you've not yet heard.   30

BAPTISTA

News that's both new and old? How can that be?

BIONDELLO

Why, isn't it news to know that Petruchio is coming?

BAPTISTA

Has he arrived?

BIONDELLO

Why, no, sir.   35

BAPTISTA

What then?

BIONDELLO

He is coming.

BAPTISTA

When will he be here?

BIONDELLO

When he stands where I am and sees you there.

TRANIO, *as* LUCENTIO

But then tell us, what's your old news?   40

BIONDELLO

Why, Petruchio is coming in a new hat and an old coat; a pair
of old pants turned inside out three times; a pair of boots that
have been candleholders, one buckled, the other laced; an old
rusty sword taken out of the town armory with a broken hilt
and no metal tip on the end of the scabbard, and with two   45
broken laces. His horse has a dislocated hip, is wearing a
moth-eaten saddle and stirrups that don't match; it also has

kindred, besides, possess'd with the glanders and like to mose in the chine, troubled with the lampass, infected with the fashions, full of windgalls, sped with spavins,

50 rayed with the yellows, past cure of the fives, stark spoil'd with the staggers, begnawn with the bots, sway'd in the back and shoulder-shotten, near-legg'd before, and with a half-check'd bit and a head stall of sheep's leather which, being restrain'd to keep him from stumbling, hath been

55 often burst and now repaired with knots; one girth six times piec'd, and a woman's crupper of velour, which hath two letters for her name fairly set down in studs, and here and there piec'd with packthread.

BAPTISTA
Who comes with him?

BIONDELLO
60 O, sir, his lackey, for all the world caparison'd like the horse: with a linen stock on one leg and a kersey boot-hose on the other, gart'red with a red and blue list; an old hat and the humour of forty fancies prick'd in 't for a feather. A monster, a very monster in apparel, and not like

65 a Christian footboy or a gentleman's lackey.

TRANIO [as LUCENTIO]
'Tis some odd humour pricks him to this fashion;
Yet oftentimes he goes but mean-apparell'd.

BAPTISTA
I am glad he's come, howsoe'er he comes.

BIONDELLO
Why, sir, he comes not.

BAPTISTA
70 Didst thou not say he comes?

BIONDELLO
Who? That Petruchio came?

BAPTISTA
Ay, that Petruchio came!

an inflamed jaw and a runny nose. It's bothered by a swollen mouth, infected with swollen glands, has tumors on its lower legs, tumors on its upper leg, is filthy from jaundice, has an incurable case of swelling behind the ears, is completely shot 50 from bad nerves, is eaten up by worms and swaybacked; has a shoulder out of joint, is knock-kneed in front; has an improperly hooked bridle, and the bridle over its head is made of sheep's leather, which has been frequently broken from being pulled to keep the horse from stumbling, and now fixed by knotting the broken parts. One belly strap has been fixed six times. The 55 strap under the tail is made out of velvet, with some woman's initials set in studs, and here and there tied with cheap thread.

BAPTISTA
Who is with him?

BIONDELLO
Oh, sir! His servant is outfitted exactly like the horse. He has a 60 linen stocking on one leg and a rough boot sock on the other. His garters have red and blue cloth hems. He's wearing an old hat that has forty weird ornaments pinned on it instead of a feather. He's a monster, a real monster in his dress—not at all like a Christian uniformed page or a gentleman's servant. 65

TRANIO, *as* LUCENTIO
It's some strange mood that leads him to go around in this
    kind of clothing.
Yet, he often walks around in shabby clothing.

BAPTISTA
I'm glad he's coming, no matter what he looks like.

BIONDELLO
Why, sir, he's not coming.

BAPTISTA
Didn't you say he was coming? 70

BIONDELLO
Who? That Petruchio was coming?

BAPTISTA
Yes, that Petruchio was coming.

BIONDELLO

No, sir, I say his horse comes with him on his back.

BAPTISTA

Why, that's all one.

BIONDELLO

75   "Nay, by Saint Jamy,
I hold you a penny,
A horse and a man
Is more than one,
And yet not many."

Enter PETRUCHIO *and* GRUMIO.

PETRUCHIO

80   Come, where be these gallants? Who's at home?

BAPTISTA

You are welcome, sir.

PETRUCHIO

And yet I come* not well.

BAPTISTA

And yet you halt not.

TRAŃIO [*as* LUCENTIO]

Not so well apparell'd

85   as I wish you were.

PETRUCHIO

Were it better, I should rush in thus—
But where is Kate? Where is my lovely bride?
How does my father? Gentles, methinks you frown.
And wherefore gaze this goodly company

90   As if they saw some wondrous monument,
Some comet or unusual prodigy?

BAPTISTA

Why, sir, you know this is your wedding day.
First were we sad, fearing you would not come;
Now sadder, that you come so unprovided.

---

82   *come* also means "walk." Baptista makes a joke on this meaning when he
remarks that Petruchio is not limping.

BIONDELLO

No, sir. I'm telling you his horse is coming, with him on the
horse's back.

BAPTISTA

Why that's the same thing.

BIONDELLO

No, not by Saint Jamy. 75
I'll bet you a penny
That a horse and a man
Is more than one
And yet not many.

> PETRUCHIO *and* GRUMIO *enter.*

PETRUCHIO

Come, where are the fancy lords? Who's at home? 80

BAPTISTA

Welcome, sir.

PETRUCHIO

And yet I don't look well.

BAPTISTA

Still, you're not limping.

TRANIO, *as* LUCENTIO

You're not as well-dressed
as I wish you were. 85

PETRUCHIO

Even if I were better dressed, I would rush in like this.
But where is Kate? Where is my lovely bride?
How are you, father-in-law? Gentlemen, I think you're frowning.
And why is this nice group staring
as if they saw some amazing omen, 90
some comet, or unusual marvel?

BAPTISTA

Why, sir, you know this is your wedding day.
First we were sad because we were afraid that you wouldn't
come.
Now we're sadder that you've come so poorly dressed.

95   Fie, doff this habit, shame to your estate,
      An eyesore to our solemn festival!

TRANIO [*as* LUCENTIO]
      And tell us, what occasion of import
      Hath all so long detain'd you from your wife,
      And sent you hither so unlike yourself?

PETRUCHIO
100   Tedious it were to tell, and harsh to hear.
      Sufficeth, I am come to keep my word,
      Though in some part enforced to **digress**;
      Which, at more leisure, I will so excuse
      As you shall well be satisfied withal.
105   The morning wears, 'tis time we were at church.

TRANIO [*as* LUCENTIO]
      See not your bride in these unreverent robes.
      Go to my chamber; put on clothes of mine.

PETRUCHIO
      Not I, believe me; thus I'll visit her.

BAPTISTA
      But thus, I trust, you will not marry her.

PETRUCHIO
110   Good sooth, even thus; therefore ha' done with words.
      To me she's married, not unto my clothes.
      Could I repair what she will wear in me,
      As I can change these poor accoutrements,
      'Twere well for Kate and better for myself.
115   But what a fool am I to chat with you,
      When I should bid good morrow to my bride
      And seal the title with a lovely kiss!

              [*Exit* PETRUCHIO *and* GRUMIO.]

TRANIO [*as* LUCENTIO]
      He hath some meaning in his mad attire.
      We will persuade him, be it possible,
120   To put on better ere he go to church.

For shame! Take off those clothes that are a disgrace to your
    position   95
and an eyesore to our solemn festival.

TRANIO, *as* LUCENTIO
And tell us what important reason
has detained you so long from joining your wife
and sent you here dressed in a style so unlike yourself?

PETRUCHIO
It would be tedious to tell and boring to listen to.   100
Let it suffice that I've come to keep my promise,
though I'm forced to abandon part of my plan.
When we have more time, I'll explain all this
to your complete satisfaction.
But where is Kate? I've been apart from her for too long.
The morning is passing, and it's time we went to church.   105

TRANIO, *as* LUCENTIO
Don't go to your bride in these ridiculous clothes.
Go to my room and put on some of my clothes.

PETRUCHIO
No, I won't. I'll see her dressed as I am.

BAPTISTA
But I trust you won't marry her in those clothes.

PETRUCHIO
So help me, just like this. So stop talking.   110
She's marrying me, not my clothes.
If I could repair what she'll wear out in me
as easily as I could change these shabby clothes,
it would be good for Kate and better for me.
But what a fool I am to chat with you   115
when I should be saying good morning to my bride
and seal my right to use that title with a loving kiss!

    Exits with GRUMIO.

TRANIO, *as* LUCENTIO
He means something by wearing those crazy clothes.
We'll try to persuade him, if it's possible,
to put on something nicer before he goes to church.   120

BAPTISTA

I'll after him, and see the event of this.

[*Exit* BAPTISTA, GREMIO, *and* ATTENDANTS.]

TRANIO

But, sir, to love* concerneth us to add
Her father's liking, which to bring to pass,
As I before imparted to your Worship,
125   I am to get a man—whate'er he be,
It skills not much, we'll fit him to our turn—
And he shall be "Vincentio of Pisa"
And make assurance here in Padua
Of greater sums that I have promised.
130   So shall you quietly enjoy your hope
And marry sweet Bianca with consent.

LUCENTIO

Were it not that my fellow schoolmaster
Doth watch Bianca's steps so narrowly,
'Twere good, methinks, to steal our marriage,
135   Which, once perform'd, let all the world say no,
I'll keep mine own, despite of all the world.

TRANIO

That by degrees we mean to look into,
And watch our vantage in this business.
We'll overreach the greybeard, Gremio,
140   The narrow prying father, Minola,
The quaint musician, amorous Litio,
All for my master's sake, Lucentio.

Reenter GREMIO.

Signior Gremio, came you from the church?

GREMIO

As willingly as e'er I came from school.

---

122   *But, sir, to love* Some scholars believe part of the play is missing here, since Tranio switches subjects so abruptly.

BAPTISTA

I'll follow him and see what happens.

Exits with GREMIO *and* ATTENDANTS.

TRANIO

But to Bianca's love we should be concerned to add
her father's approval. So to bring that about,
as I told you before, my lord,
I'll find a man—who he is   125
doesn't really matter since we'll outfit him to serve our
    purpose—
and he'll be "Vincentio from Pisa."
And he'll make settlement guarantees here in Padua
of larger sums than I promised to Baptista.
So you shall quietly fulfill your wish   130
and marry sweet Bianca with her father's consent.

LUCENTIO

If it weren't for the fact that my fellow teacher
closely watches every move Bianca makes,
I'd think it would be best to elope.
Then, once we're married, everyone in the world could
    try to stop us,   135
but I'd keep my love in spite of them.

TRANIO

We'll explore that more carefully
and guard our advantage in this business.
We'll best that greybeard, Gremio,
the suspicious and watchful father, Minola,   140
the clever musician, amorous Litio—
all for the sake of my master, Lucentio.

GREMIO enters.

Signor Gremio, have you just come from the church?

GREMIO

As eagerly as I ever came home from school.

TRANIO [*as* LUCENTIO]

145   And is the bride and bridegroom coming home?

GREMIO

A bridegroom say you? 'Tis a groom indeed,
A grumbling groom, and that the girl shall find.

TRANIO [*as* LUCENTIO]

Curster than she? Why, 'tis impossible.

GREMIO

Why, he's a devil, a devil, a very fiend.

TRANIO [*as* LUCENTIO]

150   Why, she's a devil, a devil, the devil's dam.

GREMIO

Tut, she's a lamb, a dove, a fool to him!
I'll tell you, Sir Lucentio: when the priest
Should ask if Katherine should be his wife,
"Ay, by gogs-wouns!" quoth he, and swore so loud
155   That, all amaz'd, the priest let fall the book;
And, as he stoop'd again to take it up,
The mad-brain'd bridegroom took him such a cuff
That down fell priest and book, and book and priest.
"Now take them up," quoth he, "if any list."

TRANIO [*as* LUCENTIO]

160   What said the wench when he rose again?

GREMIO

Trembled and shook, for why he stamp'd and swore
As if the vicar meant to cozen him.
But after many ceremonies done,
He calls for wine. "A health!" quoth he, as if
165   He'd been aboard, carousing to his mates
After a storm; quaff'd off the muscatel,*
And threw the sops* all in the sexton's* face,
Having no other reason

---

166   *muscatel* a sweet wine usually drunk at the end of a wedding ceremony

167   *sops* pieces of cake floating in the wine

167   *sexton* an official who takes care of a church

TRANIO, *as* LUCENTIO
And are the bride and groom coming home? 145

GREMIO
Did you say groom? He's a stable groom, indeed,
a grumbling groom, and the girl will find that out.

TRANIO, *as* LUCENTIO
He's more of a shrew than she is? Why, that's impossible!

GREMIO
Why, he's a devil, a devil, a real demon!

TRANIO, *as* LUCENTIO
Why, she's a devil, a devil, the devil's mother. 150

GREMIO
Nonsense; she's a lamb, a dove, a complete innocent compared
   to him!
I'll tell you, Sir Lucentio, when the priest
asked if Katherine would be his wife,
he said, "Ay, by God's wounds," and swore so loudly
that the priest, totally shocked, dropped the book. 155
And as he bent down to pick it up again,
this crazy bridegroom gave him such a slap
that down fell the priest and book, and the book and priest.
"Now pick them up," he said, "if anyone wants to."

TRANIO, *as* LUCENTIO
What did the woman say when he got up again? 160

GREMIO
She trembled and shook because he stomped and swore
as if the priest meant to cheat him out of his wedding.
But after all the ceremonies were completed,
he called for wine. "A toast!" he said, as if
he were on board ship, toasting his shipmates 165
after a storm. He guzzled off all the wine
and threw all the dregs in the sexton's face
for no other reason

But that his beard grew thin and hungerly,
170 And seem'd to ask him sops as he was drinking.
This done, he took the bride about the neck
And kiss'd her lips with such a **clamorous** smack
That at the parting all the church did echo.
And I, seeing this, came thence for very shame,
175 And after me, I know, the rout is coming.
Such a mad marriage never was before.

> [*Music plays.*]

Hark, hark! I hear the minstrels play.

> *Reenter* PETRUCHIO, KATHERINE, BIANCA,
> BAPTISTA, HORTENSIO, GRUMIO, TRANIO,
> *and* TRAIN.

PETRUCHIO
Gentlemen and friends, I thank you for your pains.
I know you think to dine with me today,
180 And have prepar'd great store of wedding cheer,
But so it is, my haste doth call me hence,
And therefore here I mean to take my leave.

BAPTISTA
Is 't possible you will away tonight?

PETRUCHIO
I must away today, before night come.
185 Make it no wonder; if you knew my business,
You would entreat me rather go than stay.
And, honest company, I thank you all
That have beheld me give away myself
To this most patient, sweet, and virtuous wife.
190 Dine with my father, drink a health to me,
For I must hence and farewell to you all.

TRANIO [*as* LUCENTIO]
Let us entreat you stay till after dinner.

PETRUCHIO
It may not be.

GREMIO
Let me entreat you.

than that his beard was thin and whispery
and seemed to beg for the dregs while he was drinking.   170
After he'd done this, he grabbed the bride around the neck
and kissed her lips with such a noisy smack
that when they were finished, the whole church echoed.
After I saw that, I left there out of embarrassment.
I know the crowd is at my heels.   175
There never before was such a crazy marriage!

    (*Music plays.*)

Listen, listen! I hear the musicians playing.

    PETRUCHIO, KATHERINE, BIANCA, BAPTISTA, HORTENSIO,
    GRUMIO, TRANIO, *and* GUESTS, *all enter.*

PETRUCHIO
Gentlemen and friends, I thank you for your efforts.
I know you had planned to eat with me today
and had prepared a great banquet for the wedding feast.   180
But it so happens that something urgent calls me away,
and therefore, I must say good-bye.

BAPTISTA
Do you really mean you're leaving tonight?

PETRUCHIO
I must leave today, before night falls.
Don't be surprised. If you knew my business,   185
you would beg me to go rather than to stay.
So, my good fellows, I thank everyone
who saw me give myself
to this most patient, sweet, and virtuous wife.
Go eat with my father-in-law, and drink a toast to me   190
since I must leave. Good-bye to you all.

TRANIO, *as* LUCENTIO
We beg you to stay until after dinner.

PETRUCHIO
I can't.

GREMIO
Let me beg you.

PETRUCHIO

195   It cannot be.

KATHERINE

Let me entreat you.

PETRUCHIO

I am content.

KATHERINE

Are you content to stay?

PETRUCHIO

I am content you shall entreat me stay,

200   But yet not stay, entreat me how you can.

KATHERINE

Now, if you love me, stay.

PETRUCHIO

Grumio, my horse.

GRUMIO

Ay, sir, they be ready; the oats have eaten the horses.

KATHERINE

Nay, then,

205   Do what thou canst, I will not go today;
No, nor tomorrow, not till I please myself.
The door is open, sir; there lies your way;
You may be jogging whiles your boots are green.*
For me, I'll not be gone till I please myself.

210   'Tis like you'll prove a jolly surly groom,
That take it on you at the first so roundly.

PETRUCHIO

O Kate, content thee. Prithee, be not angry.

KATHERINE

I will be angry. What hast thou to do?—
Father, be quiet; he shall stay my leisure.

GREMIO

215   Ay, marry, sir, now it begins to work.

---

208   *You . . . green.* proverbial phrase used to push unwanted guests out the door

PETRUCHIO
It's not possible.   195

KATHERINE
Let me beg you.

PETRUCHIO
I am satisfied.

KATHERINE
You mean you'll be satisfied to stay?

PETRUCHIO
I'm satisfied that you beg me to stay,
but I won't stay, no matter how you beg me.   200

KATHERINE
If you love me, let's stay.

PETRUCHIO
Grumio, get my horse!

GRUMIO
Yes, sir, they're ready. The horses are stuffed with their oats.

KATHERINE
Well, then,
do what you want. I'm not leaving today—   205
no, not tomorrow, either—until I want to go.
The door is open, sir; that's the road you're taking.
You might as well be trotting along while your boots are clean.
As for me, I won't leave until I want to.
It's likely that you'll prove an arrogant, surly groom   210
when you take charge like this at the very start.

PETRUCHIO
Oh, Kate, be content. Please don't be angry.

KATHERINE
I will be angry—what have you got to say about it?
Father, be quiet. He will wait until I'm ready to go.

GREMIO
Yes, indeed, sir—now you'll see some action.   215

KATHERINE

Gentlemen, forward to the bridal dinner.
I see a woman may be made a fool
If she had not a spirit to resist.

PETRUCHIO

They shall go forward, Kate, at thy command.—
220 Obey the bride, you that attend on her.
Go to the feast, revel and domineer,
Carouse full measure to her maidenhead,
Be mad and merry, or go hang yourselves;
But for my bonny Kate, she must with me.
225 Nay, look not big, nor stamp, nor stare, nor fret;
I will be master of what is mine own.
She is my goods, my chattels; she is my house,
My household stuff, my field, my barn,
My horse, my ox, my ass, my anything;
230 And here she stands, touch her whoever dare.
I'll bring mine action on the proudest he
That stops my way in Padua.—Grumio,
Draw forth thy weapon, we are beset with thieves;
Rescue thy mistress, if thou be a man!—
235 Fear not, sweet wench, they shall not touch thee, Kate.
I'll buckler thee against a million.

[*Exit* PETRUCHIO, KATHERINE, *and* GRUMIO.]

BAPTISTA

Nay, let them go. A couple of quiet ones!

GREMIO

Went they not quickly, I should die with laughing.

TRANIO [*as* LUCENTIO]

Of all mad matches never was the like.

LUCENTIO [*as* CAMBIO]

240 Mistress, what's your opinion of your sister?

BIANCA

That, being mad herself, she's madly mated.

KATHERINE

Gentlemen, let's go inside to the wedding feast.
I see a woman may be made a fool
if she doesn't have the spirit to put her foot down.

PETRUCHIO

They will go inside, Kate, at your command.—
Obey the bride, those of you who wait on her.   220
Go to the feast, enjoy yourselves, and kick up your heels.
Toast a full cup to her virginity,
be crazy and merry, or go hang yourselves.
But as for my good Kate, she must go with me.
No, don't look so angry, don't stomp your feet, or swagger
    or fret.   225
I will be master of what is mine.
She is my goods, my holdings. She is my house,
my household stuff, my field, my barn,
my horse, my ox, my ass, my anything.
And here she stands, whoever dares to touch her.   230
I'll bring a lawsuit against even the proudest man if he
tries to keep me here in Padua.—Grumio,
draw your weapon; we're surrounded by thieves.
Rescue your mistress, if you're a man!—
Don't be afraid, sweet woman—they'll never touch you, Kate.   235
I'll shield you from a million of them.

> PETRUCHIO, KATHERINE, *and* GRUMIO *exit.*

BAPTISTA

No, let them go, quiet couple that they are.

GREMIO

If they hadn't left as quickly as they did, I would have died
    from laughing.

TRANIO, *as* LUCENTIO

Of all the crazy couples, there never was one like those two.

LUCENTIO, *as* CAMBIO

Lady, what's your opinion of your sister?   240

BIANCA

I think that being crazy herself, she's married a crazy man.

GREMIO

I warrant him, Petruchio is Kated.

BAPTISTA

Neighbours and friends, though bride and bridegroom
wants
245   For to supply the places at the table,
You know there wants no junkets at the feast.
[*to* TRANIO] Lucentio, you shall supply the bridegroom's
place,
And let Bianca take her sister's room.

TRANIO [*as* LUCENTIO]
250   Shall sweet Bianca practise how to bride it?

BAPTISTA [*to* TRANIO]

She shall, Lucentio. Come, gentlemen, let's go.

[*Exeunt.*]

GREMIO

I guarantee you, Petruchio has already caught Kate's temper.

BAPTISTA

Neighbors and friends, though the bride and groom aren't here
to take their places at the table,   245
you know there's no lack of sweetmeats at the feast.—
Lucentio, you will fill the bridegroom's place,
and let Bianca take her sister's place.

TRANIO, *as* LUCENTIO

Is Bianca being allowed to practice how to act as a bride?   250

BAPTISTA, *as* TRANIO

She is, Lucentio. Come, gentlemen, let's go.

They exit.

Act III Review

Discussion Questions

1. What do the love scenes between Bianca and Lucentio and Bianca and Hortensio reveal about Kate's younger sister?

2. How does Kate and Petruchio's love scene contrast with Bianca's courtship?

3. How does Petruchio's delay in appearing for the wedding affect Kate?

4. What is the effect of Petruchio's shabby appearance?

5. What purpose is served by Petruchio's rude behavior at the wedding?

6. What is notable about Kate's reaction to Petruchio's announcement that they will leave before the wedding dinner?

7. What is ironic about Kate's statement "I see a woman may be made a fool / If she had not a spirit to resist"?

Literary Elements

1. **Descriptive details** create specific pictures in the mind of an audience. Find a list of descriptive details in Act III. What is the overall effect, both intentional and unintentional, of this list?

2. **Farce** is a form of comedy that is full of coincidence and ridiculous events. **Slapstick** refers to obvious physical comedy. Name some of the elements of farce and slapstick at the wedding of Petruchio and Kate.

3. An **epithet** is often a form of name-calling or insult. Find as many epithets as you can in Act III. What do you think is the purpose of all these insults?

4. A **symbol** is a person, object, action, or place that represents something beyond its obvious meaning. In Scene ii, Petruchio refuses to go to the traditional wedding feast and forces Kate to leave with him. That is the literal meaning of his speech in lines 219–236, but what is the symbolic meaning of his words and actions here?

Writing Prompts

1. Shakespeare doesn't let the audience witness Kate's and Petruchio's actual wedding. We hear about it from the outraged Gremio. Pretend you are a society reporter and write up an account of this ceremony for the local newspaper.

2. Write a soliloquy in Elizabethan language giving Kate's reaction to Petruchio's behavior at their wedding.

3. Write a series of diary entries by Kate that lead up to her wedding to Petruchio.

4. Reread Petruchio's speech to Kate in Act III, Scene ii, lines 219–236. Here, he tells his new wife that she cannot attend her own bridal dinner ("I will be master of what is mine own."). Now rewrite it from a woman's point of view, using a man's name and different details. What is the effect?

5. Reread the description of Petruchio's wedding apparel (Scene ii, lines 41–45). Modern readers probably have to look up many of the details to understand this description. Write a similar list describing the apparel you would want to wear to your own wedding, perhaps one that would puzzle a person from Shakespeare's day.

The Taming of the Shrew

ACT IV

Josie Lawrence as Katherine and Michael Siberry as Petruchio, Royal Shakespeare Company, 1995

"This is a way to kill a wife
with kindness."

Before You Read

1. Be ready for the change in Kate's attitude toward Petruchio. Take note of all the things Petruchio does to influence her.

2. Depending on the way it is staged, Act IV contains a lot of physical violence (or slapstick) and verbal insults (or comic wordplay). Note your personal reaction to Petruchio's efforts to "tame" Kate.

3. At this point in the story, what is your opinion of Lucentio? Explain why.

Literary Elements

1. A **metaphor** makes a direct comparison between unlike things, which nevertheless may share some common features. At the wedding in Act III, Gremio compares Petruchio to the devil ("he's a devil, a devil, a very fiend") and Kate to a "lamb" and a "fool" by contrast with her new husband.

2. An **extended metaphor** compares two unlike things at some length and in various ways. In Act II, Scene i, Petruchio makes a lengthy comparison between himself and Kate courting ("two raging fires" that come together and "consume the thing that feeds their fury").

3. **Conflict**, or struggle between opposing forces, is what creates tension and drama in a piece of writing. *The Taming of the Shrew* is a play about the conflict between men and women, as characterized by the strong, well-matched personalities of Petruchio and Kate.

4. A **soliloquy** is a longer speech that reveals the innermost thoughts and feelings of the character who speaks it. One of Shakespeare's most well-known soliloquies is Hamlet's "to-be-or-not-to-be" speech.

Words to Know

The following vocabulary words appear in Act IV in the original text of Shakespeare's play. However, they are words that are still used today. Read the definitions here, and pay attention to the words as you read the play (they will be in boldfaced type).

austerity	seriousness; dignity
allots	gives; assigns
credulous	trusting; believing
diligent	attentive; thoughtful
dissemble	lie; hedge the truth
engenders	produces; creates
expound	explain; elaborate on
oblivion	forgotten; unremembered
paltry	trivial; worthless
renowned	famous; well-known

Act Summary

Grumio relates to Curtis, another servant, the shocking behavior of the newlyweds on the journey to their country home. Petruchio beat and humiliated Grumio and allowed Kate to lie in the mud after a fall from her horse.

When they arrive, Petruchio steps up his campaign of abuse, ranting and railing at the servants, throwing food, and ignoring Kate's pleas to behave decently. After the others leave, he reveals his plan for his unruly wife: She will get no food or drink or sleep. Like a wild falcon, she will be tamed.

Hortensio decides to marry the rich Widow, realizing that Bianca is more interested in her tutor, Cambio (really Lucentio). Still posing as his master, Tranio finds the Pedant and tells him a lie in order to convince him to pose as Vincentio. The Pedant is happy to accept, thinking his life is endangered.

Raul Julia and Meryl Streep, Delacorte Theatre, 1978

Petruchio wears Kate down with his tricks. When her new outfit for Bianca's wedding is delivered, he flies into a rage and throws it on the floor. He contradicts the time of day and then demands that she agree with him.

Tranio and the Pedant, in their disguises as Lucentio and Vincentio, go to Baptista and agree to the dowry. Meanwhile a priest awaits the real Lucentio and Bianca, who have decided to elope after hearing that Baptista has agreed to their marriage.

On the way to Padua and the wedding feast, Petruchio makes further demands on Kate's spirit. He wants her total obedience: If he calls the sun the moon, she must agree. They meet an elderly man on the road, who Petruchio claims is a fair young maiden. No longer wanting to disagree, Kate addresses the old man as if he were a young girl. Then Petruchio changes his mind again, and true to her word, Kate remains in agreement with him. The man joins them and reveals that he is Vincentio, Lucentio's father.

ACT IV, SCENE I

[Petruchio's country house.] Enter GRUMIO.

GRUMIO
Fie, fie on all tired jades, on all mad masters, and all foul
ways! Was ever man so beaten? Was ever man so 'rayed?
Was ever man so weary? I am sent before to make a fire,
and they are coming after to warm them. Now, were not I
5   a little pot and soon hot,* my very lips might freeze to my
teeth, my tongue to the roof of my mouth, my heart in my
belly, ere I should come by a fire to thaw me. But I, with
blowing the fire, shall warm myself; for, considering the
weather, a taller man than I will take cold.—Holla, ho!
10 Curtis.

Enter CURTIS.

CURTIS
Who is that calls so coldly?

GRUMIO
A piece of ice. If thou doubt it, thou mayst slide from my
shoulder to my heel with no greater a run but my head
and my neck. A fire, good Curtis!

CURTIS
15 Is my master and his wife coming, Grumio?

GRUMIO
O, ay, Curtis, ay, and therefore fire, fire! Cast on no water.

CURTIS
Is she so hot a shrew as she's reported?

GRUMIO
She was, good Curtis, before this frost. But thou know'st,
winter tames man, woman, and beast, for it hath tam'd
20 my old master and my new mistress and myself, fellow
Curtis.

---

5   *a little pot and soon hot* a proverb meaning that small people have quick tempers

ACT 4, SCENE 1

PETRUCHIO'S *country house.* GRUMIO *enters.*

GRUMIO
Damn all tired nags, all crazy masters, and all muddy roads!
Was there ever a man as beaten as I've been? Was there ever
a man as muddy? Was there ever a man as weary? I'm sent
ahead to make a fire, and they'll arrive later to warm
themselves. Well, if I wasn't a little kettle and quick to get
boiling mad, my lips might freeze to my teeth, my tongue to   5
the roof of my mouth, my heart in my belly before I could
reach a fire to thaw myself. But I, by blowing the fire, will
warm myself. Considering the weather, a tougher man than
I am would catch cold.—Hello, hello! Curtis!   10

CURTIS *enters.*

CURTIS
Who is calling in that shaking voice?

GRUMIO
A piece of ice. If you doubt my word, you can slide from my
shoulder to my heel with no more of a running start than my
head and neck. A fire, good Curtis!

CURTIS
Are my master and his wife coming, Grumio?   15

GRUMIO
Oh, yes, Curtis, yes. Therefore, make a fire, a fire! Don't throw
any water on it.

CURTIS
Is she as hot-tempered a shrew as she's reported to be?

GRUMIO
She was, good Curtis, before this frost. But you know that
winter tames man, woman, and beast. And it has tamed my
old master, my new mistress, and me, fellow Curtis.   20

CURTIS

Away, you three-inch fool!* I am no beast.

GRUMIO

Am I but three inches? Why, thy horn* is a foot; and so
long am I at the least. But wilt thou make a fire, or shall I
complain on thee to our mistress, whose hand, she being
now at hand, thou shalt soon feel, to thy cold comfort, for
being slow in thy hot office?

CURTIS

I prithee, good Grumio, tell me, how goes the world?

GRUMIO

A cold world, Curtis, in every office but thine, and
therefore fire! Do thy duty, and have thy duty, for my
master and mistress are almost frozen to death.

CURTIS

There's fire ready. And therefore, good Grumio, the news!

GRUMIO

Why, "Jack, boy! Ho! boy!"* and as much news as wilt thou.

CURTIS

Come, you are so full of cony-catching!

GRUMIO

Why, therefore fire, for I have caught extreme cold.
Where's the cook? Is supper ready, the house trimm'd,
rushes strew'd, cobwebs swept, the servingmen in their
new fustian, their white stockings, and every officer his
wedding garment on? Be the Jacks* fair within, the Jills*
fair without, the carpets laid, and everything in order?

CURTIS

All ready. And therefore, I pray thee, news.

---

22   *three-inch fool* Curtis is commenting on Grumio's shortness and also making a
phallic joke.

23   *horn* the sign of a cuckold (a man whose wife was an adulteress)

33   *Jack . . . boy!* a line from a familiar song

39   *Jacks* means both "male servants" and "leather drinking cups"

39   *Jills* means both "female servants" and "metal drinking cups smaller than a jack"

CURTIS

Go away, you three-inch fool! I'm not an animal.

GRUMIO

So I'm just three inches? Why, your horn is a foot long, and I'm at least that long. But will you make a fire, or shall I complain about you to our mistress, whose hand—and she's coming 25 shortly—you shall soon feel to your cold discomfort if you're slow about your job of making a fire?

CURTIS

I beg you, good Grumio, tell me what's going on in the world.

GRUMIO

A cold world, Curtis, in every respect except yours and therefore, make a fire. Do your duty, and receive your reward 30 because my master and mistress are almost frozen to death.

CURTIS

The fire is ready. Therefore, good Grumio, let's have the news.

GRUMIO

Why, "Jack, boy! Ho, boy!" and whatever news you want.

CURTIS

Come on, you're too full of mischief.

GRUMIO

Well then, make a fire, because I'm extremely cold. Where's the 35 cook? Is supper ready, the house tidy, rushes scattered on the floor, the cobwebs swept away, all the menials in their best working clothes and white stockings, and every servant with his wedding uniform on? Are the men inside tidy, the maids well dressed, the tablecloths laid, and everything in order? 40

CURTIS

Everything is ready. Therefore, please tell me the news.

GRUMIO

First, know, my horse is tired, my master and mistress
fall'n out.

CURTIS

How?

GRUMIO

45 Out of their saddles into the dirt, and thereby hangs a tale.

CURTIS

Let's ha 't, good Grumio.

GRUMIO

Lend thine ear.

CURTIS

Here.

GRUMIO

There.

[*Strikes him.*]

CURTIS

50 This is to feel a tale, not to hear a tale.

GRUMIO

And therefore 'tis call'd a sensible* tale, and this cuff was
but to knock at your ear, and beseech list'ning. Now I
begin: *Imprimis,** we came down a foul hill, my master
riding behind my mistress—

CURTIS

55 Both of one horse?

GRUMIO

What's that to thee?

CURTIS

Why, a horse.

GRUMIO

Tell thou the tale! But hadst thou not cross'd me, thou
shouldst have heard how her horse fell and she under her

---

51 *sensible* means both "reasonable" and "able to be sensed or felt"

53 *Imprimis* Latin for "first"

GRUMIO

First, I'll tell you that my horse is tired. And my master and mistress have had a falling out.

CURTIS

What?

GRUMIO

Out of their saddles and into the dirt—and thereby hangs a tale. 45

CURTIS

Let's hear it, good Grumio.

GRUMIO

Then lend an ear.

CURTIS

Here it is.

GRUMIO

There.

>   *Strikes him.*

CURTIS

This is feeling a tale, not hearing one. 50

GRUMIO

And that's why it's called a sensible tale. That blow was just to knock at your ear and beg you to listen. Now I'll start: First, we came down a muddy hill, my master riding behind my mistress—

CURTIS

Both of them on one horse? 55

GRUMIO

What's that to you?

CURTIS

Why, a horse.

GRUMIO

Then you tell the story. But if you hadn't interrupted, you would have heard how her horse fell, and she fell under the

60 horse; thou shouldst have heard in how miry a place, how
she was bemoil'd, how he left her with the horse upon
her, how he beat me because her horse stumbled, how she
waded through the dirt to pluck him off me, how he
swore, how she pray'd that never pray'd before, how I
65 cried, how the horses ran away, how her bridle was burst,
how I lost my crupper, with many things of worthy
memory which now shall die in **oblivion** and thou return
unexperienc'd to thy grave.

CURTIS
By this reck'ning, he is more shrew than she.

GRUMIO
70 Ay, and that thou and the proudest of you all shall find
when he comes home. But what talk I of this? Call forth
Nathaniel, Joseph, Nicholas, Phillip, Walter, Sugarsop and
the rest. Let their heads be slickly comb'd, their blue coats
brush'd and their garters of an indifferent knit; let them
75 curtsy with their left legs and not presume to touch a hair
of my master's horsetail till they kiss their hands. Are they
all ready?

CURTIS
They are.

GRUMIO
Call them forth.

CURTIS [*calling out*]
80 Do you hear, ho? You must meet my master to
countenance* my mistress.

GRUMIO
Why, she hath a face of her own.

CURTIS
Who knows not that?

GRUMIO
Thou, it seems, that calls for company to countenance her.

CURTIS
85 I call them forth to credit her.

---

81 *countenance* means both "show respect to" and "face"

horse. You would have heard how muddy the place was where 60
she fell, how she was covered in mud, how he let her lie there
with the horse on top of her, how he beat me because her
horse had stumbled, how she waded through the mud to pull
him off of me, how he swore, how she prayed when she'd
never prayed before, how I cried, how the horses ran away, 65
how her bridle broke, and how I lost my horse's tail strap. All
this and many other memorable things will now die unheard
and you go to your grave none the wiser.

CURTIS

By your tale, he's more of a shrew than she is.

GRUMIO

Yes, and you and the proudest one of the servants will find 70
that out when he comes home. But why am I talking about
this? Call Nathaniel, Joseph, Nicholas, Phillip, Walter, Sugarsop,
and the rest. See that their hair is slickly combed, their blue
coats brushed, and that they're wearing proper garters. See
that they bow with their left legs and don't dare touch a hair 75
of my master's horse's tail until they have kissed their lord's
and lady's hands. Is everyone ready?

CURTIS

They are.

GRUMIO

Call them here.

CURTIS

Did you hear that? Come! You must meet my master to present 80
my mistress with a respectful face.

GRUMIO

Why, she has a face of her own.

CURTIS

Who doesn't know that?

GRUMIO

You, it seems, who ask for the servants to face her.

CURTIS

I summoned them to pay their respects to her. 85

GRUMIO

Why, she comes to borrow nothing of them.

Enter four or five SERVINGMEN.

NATHANIEL

Welcome home, Grumio!

PHILLIP

How now, Grumio!

JOSEPH

What, Grumio!

NICHOLAS

90   Fellow Grumio.

NATHANIEL

How now, old lad?

GRUMIO

Welcome, you!—How now, you?—What, you!—Fellow, you!—And thus much for greeting. Now, my spruce companions, is all ready, and all things neat?

NATHANIEL

95   All things is ready. How near is our master?

GRUMIO

E'en at hand, alighted by this. And therefore be not—Cock's passion, silence! I hear my master.

Enter PETRUCHIO *and* KATHERINE.

PETRUCHIO

Where be these knaves? What, no man at door
To hold my stirrup nor to take my horse?
100   Where is Nathaniel, Gregory, Phillip?

ALL SERVANTS

Here! Here, sir, here, sir!

PETRUCHIO

"Here, sir! Here, sir! Here, sir! Here, sir!"
You loggerheaded and unpolish'd grooms!
What, no attendance? No regard? No duty?
105   Where is the foolish knave I sent before?

GRUMIO
Why, she hasn't come here to borrow anything from them!

Four or five SERVANTS *enter.*

NATHANIEL
Welcome home, Grumio!

PHILLIP
How are you doing, Grumio!

JOSEPH
What's up, Grumio!

NICHOLAS
My good fellow, Grumio.   90

NATHANIEL
How are you, old lad!

GRUMIO
Welcome to you!—How are you doing?—What's up with you?—
My good fellow to you!—And that's all for greetings. Now, my tidy
friends, is everything ready and everything prepared?

NATHANIEL
Everything is ready. How near is our master?   95

GRUMIO
He's nearly here; dismounted by now. Therefore, don't be—by God,
quiet! I hear my master.

PETRUCHIO *and* KATHERINE *enter.*

PETRUCHIO
Where are those rascals? What! No man at the door,
to hold my stirrup or take my horse?
Where is Nathaniel, Gregory, and Phillip?   100

ALL SERVANTS
Here! Here, sir, here, sir!

PETRUCHIO
"Here, sir! Here, sir! Here, sir! Here, sir!"
You blockheaded and clumsy grooms!
What, no service? No respect? Not doing your duty?
Where is that foolish rascal I sent ahead of me?   105

GRUMIO

Here, sir, as foolish as I was before.

PETRUCHIO

You peasant swain! You whoreson malt-horse* drudge!
Did I not bid thee meet me in the park,
And bring along these rascal knaves with thee?

GRUMIO

110 Nathaniel's coat, sir, was not fully made,
And Gabriel's pumps were all unpink'd i' th' heel.
There was no link* to colour Peter's hat,
And Walter's dagger was not come from sheathing.
There were none fine but Adam, Ralph, and Gregory.
115 The rest were ragged, old, and beggarly.
Yet, as they are, here are they come to meet you.

PETRUCHIO

Go, rascals, go, and fetch my supper in!

[*Exeunt* SERVANTS.]

[*Singing.*] "Where is the life that late I led?*
Where are those"—Sit down, Kate, and welcome.—
120 Soud, soud, soud, soud!*

Reenter SERVANTS *with supper.*

Why, when, I say?—Nay, good sweet Kate, be merry.—
Off with my boots, you rogues! You villains, when?
[*Sings.*] "It was the friar of orders gray,
As he forth walked on his way"—*
125 Out, you rogue! You pluck my foot awry.
Take that!   [*He hits the servant.*]
And mend the plucking of the other.—
Be merry, Kate.—Some water, here! What, ho!

---

107   *malt-horse* a type of slow and heavy workhorse used on a brewery treadmill

112   *link* or torch; the soot from torches was used to blacken hats

118   "*Where . . . led!*" line from an old ballad

120   *Soud* the meaning of the word is debated. Some scholars believe it is an
exclamation expressing impatience. Others believe the word really should
read "food."

123–24   "*It . . . way*" a line from another old song

GRUMIO

Here, sir. Just as foolish as I was before.

PETRUCHIO

You peasant rustic! You worthless brewery horse!
Didn't I tell you to meet me outside
and bring along those rascally scamps with you?

GRUMIO

Nathaniel's coat was not completely finished,   110
and Gabriel's shoes were not decorated with punched holes
    at the heel.
There was no torch to color Peter's hat,
and Walter's dagger scabbard hasn't been repaired yet.
No one was presentable, except Adam, Ralph, and Gregory.
The rest were ragged, old, and looked like beggars.   115
Yet, even with their flaws, they come here to meet you.

PETRUCHIO

Go, rascals, go and bring my supper.

      SERVANTS *exit.*

(Sings.) *Where is the life that late I led?*
Where are those—Sit down, Kate. Welcome.—
Food, food, food, food!   120

      SERVANTS *enter with supper.*

Well, when are you going to bring it in?—No, good, sweet Kate,
    be happy—
Take off my boots, you rascals, you peasants! Service!
(Sings.) *It was a friar of the grey brotherhood,*
who walked onward on his way.—
Stop, you rascal! You're pulling my foot the wrong way!   125
Take that, and do better with pulling the other foot!

    Strikes him.

Be happy, Kate.—Bring some water, here. Speed it up!

Enter one with water.

Where's my spaniel Troilus? Sirrah, get you hence,
130 And bid my cousin Ferdinand come hither. [*A* SERVANT *exits.*]
One, Kate, that you must kiss, and be acquainted with.—
Where are my slippers? Shall I have some water?—
Come, Kate, and wash, and welcome heartily.—
You whoreson villain! Will you let it fall?

[*Strikes the* SERVANT.]

KATHERINE
135 Patience, I pray you, 'twas a fault unwilling.

PETRUCHIO
A whoreson beetle-headed,* flap-ear'd knave!—
Come, Kate, sit down; I know you have a stomach.*
Will you give thanks, sweet Kate; or else shall I?—
What's this? Mutton?

1. SERVANT
140 Ay.

PETRUCHIO
Who brought it?

PETER
I.

PETRUCHIO
'Tis burnt, and so is all the meat.
What dogs are these? Where is the rascal cook?
145 How durst you, villains, bring it from the dresser,
And serve it thus to me that love it not?
There, take it to you, trenchers, cups, and all.

[*Throws the food and dishes about the stage.*]

You heedless joltheads and unmanner'd slaves!
What, do you grumble? I'll be with you straight.

---

136 *beetle-headed* a beetle was a wooden mallet

137 *stomach* means both "appetite" and "hot temper"

A SERVANT *enters carrying water.*

Where's my spaniel Troilus? Servant, go
and tell my cousin Ferdinand to come here. 130

SERVANT *exits.*

He's a person, Kate, that you must kiss and get to know.—
Where are my slippers? Will you give me some water?—
Come, Kate, and wash. You're heartily welcome.—
You shiftless peasant! So you'll drop it, will you?

Strikes him.

KATHERINE
Please show a little patience. He didn't mean to drop it. 135

PETRUCHIO
A shiftless, stupid, floppy-eared rascal!—
Come, Kate, sit down. I know you have an appetite.
Will you say grace, sweet Kate, or should I?—
What's this? Mutton?

FIRST SERVANT
Yes. 140

PETRUCHIO
Who brought it?

PETER
I did.

PETRUCHIO
It's burnt. And so is all the rest of the meat.
These fellows are dogs! Where is that rascal of a cook?
How dare you, you peasants, bring it from the sideboard 145
and serve it like this to me when I dislike it?
There! Take it away—the platters, cups, everything!

Throws the meat and dishes about.

You dim-witted idiots and uncouth slaves!
What! Are you griping? I'll settle your hash right now!

KATHERINE

150   I pray you, husband, be not so disquiet.
    The meat was well, if you were so contented.

PETRUCHIO

    I tell thee, Kate, 'twas burnt and dried away,
    And I expressly am forbid to touch it,
    For it **engenders** choler, planteth anger;
155   And better 'twere that both of us did fast,
    Since of ourselves, ourselves are choleric,
    Than feed it with such over-roasted flesh.
    Be patient; tomorrow 't shall be mended.
    And, for this night, we'll fast for company.
160   Come, I will bring thee to thy bridal chamber.

    [*Exeunt.*]

    Enter SERVANTS *severally.*

NATHANIEL

    Peter, didst ever see the like?

PETER

    He kills her in her own humour.

    Reenter CURTIS, *a servant.*

GRUMIO

    Where is he?

CURTIS

    In her chamber, making a sermon of continency to her,
165   And rails and swears and rates, that she, poor soul,
    Knows not which way to stand, to look, to speak,
    And sits as one new-risen from a dream.
    Away, away, for he is coming hither!

    [*Exeunt.*]

    Reenter PETRUCHIO.

PETRUCHIO

    Thus have I politicly begun my reign,
170   And 'tis my hope to end successfully.

KATHERINE

Please, husband, don't get so upset.   150
The meat was tasty, if you had just been willing to try it.

PETRUCHIO

I tell you, Kate, it was burnt and completely dry.
And I'm specifically forbidden to eat dry meat
since it brings about bad temper and raises anger.
So it would be better if both of us fasted,   155
since we ourselves are hot-tempered,
rather than feed our tempers with that burned meat.
Be patient. Tomorrow we'll make up for it.
Tonight we'll fast together.
Come, I'll take you to your bridal room.   160

>   KATE *and* PETRUCHIO *exit.*

>   *Several* SERVANTS *enter from different directions.*

NATHANIEL

Peter, did you ever see the likes of that?

PETER

He's taming her with her own medicine.

>   CURTIS *and a* SERVANT *enter.*

GRUMIO

Where is he?

CURTIS

In her room, giving her a sermon on abstaining.
And he rants and swears and berates her so much that she,   165
    poor soul,
doesn't know which way to stand, or look, or speak.
She sits like someone just awakened from a dream.
Hide, hide! He's coming here.

>   *They exit.*

>   PETRUCHIO *enters.*

PETRUCHIO

I have begun my reign shrewdly
and I hope to end successfully.   170

My falcon* now is sharp and passing empty,
And till she stoop* she must not be full-gorg'd,
For then she never looks upon her lure.*
Another way I have to man my haggard,
175   To make her come and know her keeper's call,
That is, to watch her, as we watch these kites*
That bate and beat and will not be obedient.
She ate no meat today, nor none shall eat;
Last night* she slept not, nor tonight she shall not;
180   As with the meat, some undeserved fault
I'll find about the making of the bed;
And here I'll fling the pillow, there the bolster,
This way the coverlet, another way the sheets.
Ay, and amid this hurly I intend
185   That all is done in reverend care of her.
And, in conclusion, she shall watch all night,
And if she chance to nod, I'll rail and brawl,
And with the clamour keep her still awake.
This is a way to kill a wife with kindness.
190   And thus I'll curb her mad and headstrong humour.
He that knows better how to tame a shrew,
Now let him speak; 'tis charity to shew.

       [*Exit.*]

---

171   *falcon* a hawk trained to hunt

172   *stoop* means both "obey" and "a falcon's swoop to seize prey"

173   *lure* bait that a falconer uses to get the falcon to return

176   *kites* small hawks

179   *last night* This seems to be a mistake; this scene occurs the night of the wedding.

My falcon is now starved and very empty,
and until she's tamed, she must not have a full meal
because then she'll never be tempted by the bait.
I have another way to tame my unruly female hawk,
to make her come and recognize her keeper's command,   175
and that is to keep her up, like a kite is kept from sleeping
when it flutters and beats its wings and won't obey.
She ate no meat today, and she won't be given any.
She didn't sleep last night, and she won't tonight.
As I did with the meat, I'll pretend to find something wrong   180
with the way the bed is made.
I'll fling a pillow here, a bolster there;
toss the coverlet this way, the sheets in another direction.
Yes, and while I'm creating all this fuss, I'll pretend
that I'm doing it all out of respectful care for her.   185
In short, she'll be up all night;
and if she should start to nod off, I'll rant and rave
and keep her awake with the noise.
This is the way to kill a wife with kindness,
and the way I'll tame her crazy, headstrong temper.   190
The man who knows how to tame a shrew better than this,
let him speak now—it would be an act of kindness to tell how.

    Exit.

ACT IV, SCENE II

[*Padua. Before Baptista's house.*] *Enter* TRANIO, *as* LUCENTIO, *and* HORTENSIO, *as* LITIO.

TRANIO [*as* LUCENTIO]
Is 't possible, friend Litio, that Mistress Bianca
Doth fancy any other but Lucentio?
I tell you, sir, she bears me fair in hand.

HORTENSIO [*as* LITIO]
Sir, to satisfy you in what I have said,
5   Stand by and mark the manner of his teaching.

Enter BIANCA *and* LUCENTIO, *as* CAMBIO.

LUCENTIO [*as* CAMBIO]
Now, mistress, profit you in what you read?

BIANCA
What, master, read you? First resolve me that.

LUCENTIO [*as* CAMBIO]
I read that I profess, *The Art of Love.**

BIANCA
And may you prove, sir, master of your art!

LUCENTIO [*as* CAMBIO]
10   While you, sweet dear, prove mistress of my heart!

[*They move aside and kiss and talk.*]

HORTENSIO [*as* LITIO]
Quick proceeders, marry! Now, tell me, I pray,
You that durst swear that your mistress Bianca
Lov'd none in the world so well as Lucentio.

TRANIO [*as* LUCENTIO]
O despiteful love! Unconstant womankind!
15   I tell thee, Litio, this is wonderful.

---

8   *The Art of Love*   a treatise on love by Ovid

ACT 4, SCENE 2

Padua. Before BAPTISTA's *house.* TRANIO (*as* LUCENTIO) *and* HORTENSIO (*as* LITIO) *enter.*

TRANIO, *as* LUCENTIO
Is it possible, my friend Licio, that Lady Bianca
can like anyone except Lucentio?
I tell you, sir, she seems to lead me on.

HORTENSIO, *as* LITIO
Sir, to assure you that what I said was true,
stand aside and watch how he conducts himself when he
teaches.   5

They stand aside.

BIANCA *and* LUCENTIO (*as* CAMBIO) *enter.*

LUCENTIO, *as* CAMBIO
Now, my lady, do you learn anything from what you read?

BIANCA
What are you reading, master? First tell me that.

LUCENTIO, *as* CAMBIO
I read what I preach, *The Art of Love.*

BIANCA
And may you prove to be a master of your art, sir!

LUCENTIO, *as* CAMBIO
While you, my dear sweet, prove yourself mistress of my heart.   10

They kiss and talk.

HORTENSIO, *as* LITIO
Fast workers, indeed! Now what do you say, I ask you—
you who dared swear that your lady Bianca
loved no one in the world as well as Lucentio?

TRANIO, *as* LUCENTIO
Oh spiteful love! Fickle women!
I tell you, Litio, this is shocking!   15

HORTENSIO

    Mistake no more; I am not Litio,
    Nor a musician, as I seem to be,
    But one that scorn to live in this disguise
    For such a one as leaves a gentleman
20   And makes a god of such a cullion.
    Know, sir, that I am call'd Hortensio.

TRANIO [*as* LUCENTIO]

    Signior Hortensio, I have often heard
    Of your entire affection to Bianca;
    And since mine eyes are witness of her lightness,
25   I will with you, if you be so contented,
    Forswear Bianca and her love forever.

HORTENSIO

    See how they kiss and court! Signior Lucentio,
    Here is my hand, and here I firmly vow
    Never to woo her more, but do forswear her
30   As one unworthy all the former favours
    That I have fondly flatter'd her withal.

TRANIO [*as* LUCENTIO]

    And here I take the like unfeigned oath,
    Never to marry with her though she would entreat.
    Fie on her! See, how beastly she doth court him!

HORTENSIO

35   Would all the world but he had quite forsworn!
    For me, that I may surely keep mine oath,
    I will be married to a wealthy widow
    Ere three days pass, which hath as long lov'd me
    As I have lov'd this proud disdainful haggard.
40   And so farewell, Signior Lucentio.
    Kindness in women, not their beauteous looks,
    Shall win my love; and so I take my leave,
    In resolution as I swore before.

        [*Exit.*]

TRANIO

    Mistress Bianca, bless you with such grace
45   As 'longeth to a lover's blessed case!
    Nay, I have ta'en you napping, gentle love,

HORTENSIO
Don't be fooled, anymore. I'm not Litio,
or a musician, as I appear to be,
but someone who despises keeping up this disguise
for a woman who deserts a gentleman
and worships such a crude fellow. 20
Sir, know that my name is Hortensio.

TRANIO, *as* LUCENTIO
Signor Hortensio, I've often heard
about your complete devotion to Bianca.
And since I witnessed for myself her fickleness,
I'll join with you, if you're agreeable, 25
in swearing off Bianca and her love forever.

HORTENSIO
Look at how they're kissing and courting. Signor Lucentio,
here's my hand, and here I swear
never to court her again. I reject her
as someone who is unworthy of all the respect 30
that I foolishly paid her in everything before.

TRANIO, *as* LUCENTIO
And here I'll take the same sincere vow
never to marry her, even though she begged me.
Damn her! Just look at how blatantly she courts him.

HORTENSIO
If only she had just one lover! 35
As for me, so that I may be sure to keep my vow,
I'll marry a wealthy widow
before three days have gone by. She has loved me as long
as I've loved this proud, uppity, untamed hawk.
Well, good-bye, Signor Lucentio. 40
Now kindness in women, not a beautiful appearance,
will win my love. So, I'll leave you
with the vow I just swore to you.

> *Exit.*

TRANIO (*to* BIANCA)
Lady Bianca, may you be blessed with the kind of grace
as suits a lover's happy state! 45
Oh yes, I've seen your love-play, gentle lover,

And have forsworn you with Hortensio.

BIANCA

Tranio, you jest. But have you both forsworn me?

TRANIO

Mistress, we have.

LUCENTIO

50   Then we are rid of Litio.

TRANIO

I' faith, he'll have a lusty widow now
That shall be woo'd and wedded in a day.

BIANCA

God give him joy!

TRANIO

Ay, and he'll tame her.

BIANCA

55   He says so, Tranio?

TRANIO

Faith, he is gone unto the taming school.

BIANCA

The taming school! What, is there such a place?

TRANIO

Ay, mistress, and Petruchio is the master;
That teacheth tricks eleven and twenty long*
60   To tame a shrew and charm her chattering tongue.

          Enter BIONDELLO.

BIONDELLO

O master, master, I have watch'd so long
That I am dog-weary, but at last I spied
An ancient angel* coming down the hill,
Will serve the turn.

TRANIO

65   What is he, Biondello?

---

59   *tricks eleven and twenty long*   This may be a reference to the card game *trentuno*,
     in which a player who took thirty-one tricks won the game.

63   *angel*   an old, valued coin

and I've forsaken you, as has Hortensio.

BIANCA
Tranio, you're joking. Have both of you really deserted me?

TRANIO
We have, lady.

LUCENTIO
Then we're rid of Litio. 50

TRANIO
Yes, really. He'll marry a lively widow, now,
whom he'll court and marry in the same day.

BIANCA
God make him happy!

TRANIO
Yes, if he'll tame her.

BIANCA
He says he will, Tranio? 55

TRANIO
Indeed, he's gone to the taming school.

BIANCA
The taming school! What! Is there such a place?

TRANIO
Yes, lady, and Petruchio is the teacher
who teaches winning tricks
to tame a shrew and quiet her nagging tongue. 60

　　　　BIONDELLO *enters.*

BIONDELLO
Oh master, master! I've been watching for so long
that I'm dead-tired, but I finally spotted
a trusty old soul coming down the hill
who will do the trick.

TRANIO
Who is he, Biondello? 65

BIONDELLO

Master, a marcantant, or a pedant,
I know not what; but formal in apparel,
In gait and countenance surely like a father.

LUCENTIO

And what of him, Tranio?

TRANIO

70   If he be **credulous** and trust my tale,
I'll make him glad to seem Vincentio,
And give assurance to Baptista Minola
As if he were the right Vincentio.
Take in your love, and then let me alone.

[Exeunt LUCENTIO *and* BIANCA.]

Enter a PEDANT.

PEDANT

75   God save you, sir!

TRANIO [*as* LUCENTIO]

                And you sir! You are welcome.
Travel you far on, or are you at the farthest?

PEDANT

Sir, at the farthest for a week or two,
But then up farther, and as far as Rome,
80   And so to Tripoli, if God lend me life.

TRANIO [*as* LUCENTIO]

What countryman, I pray?

PEDANT

                      Of Mantua.

TRANIO [*as* LUCENTIO]

Of Mantua, sir? Marry, God forbid!
And come to Padua, careless of your life?

PEDANT

85   My life, sir! How, I pray? For that goes hard.

BIONDELLO
Master, either a merchant or a teacher,
I'm not sure. But he dresses formally,
and in the way he carries himself and behaves, he's just like a
  father.

LUCENTIO
And what do you plan to do, Tranio?

TRANIO
If he's trusting and believes my story,   70
I'll make him happy to pretend to be Vincentio
and give guarantees to Baptista Minola
just as if he were the real Vincentio.
Take your lover inside and leave me to see to this business.

> LUCENTIO *and* BIANCA *exit.*

> PEDANT *enters.*

PEDANT
God bless you, sir!   75

TRANIO, *as* LUCENTIO
And you, too, sir! Greetings.
Are you traveling farther, or have you reached your destination?

PEDANT
Sir, I'll stay here for a week or two,
but then I'll go on as far as Rome
and then to Tripoli, if I live that long.   80

TRANIO, *as* LUCENTIO
Where are you from, if I may ask?

PEDANT
From Mantua.

TRANIO, *as* LUCENTIO
From Mantua, sir! Indeed, God forbid!
And you came to Padua, so recklessly risking your life?

PEDANT
My life, sir! What do you mean? That's rough news!   85

TRANIO [*as* LUCENTIO]
'Tis death for anyone in Mantua
To come to Padua. Know you not the cause?
Your ships are stay'd at Venice, and the Duke,
For private quarrel 'twixt your duke and him,
90   Hath publish'd and proclaim'd it openly.
'Tis marvel, but that you are but newly come,
You might have heard it else proclaim'd about.

PEDANT
Alas! Sir, it is worse for me than so,
For I have bills for money by exchange
95   From Florence, and must here deliver them.

TRANIO [*as* LUCENTIO]
Well, sir, to do you courtesy,
This will I do, and this I will advise you.
First, tell me, have you ever been at Pisa?

PEDANT
Ay, sir, in Pisa have I often been,
100   Pisa **renowned** for grave citizens.

TRANIO [*as* LUCENTIO]
Among them know you one Vincentio?

PEDANT
I know him not, but I have heard of him:
A merchant of incomparable wealth.

TRANIO [*as* LUCENTIO]
He is my father, sir, and, sooth to say,
105   In count'nance somewhat doth resemble you.

BIONDELLO [*aside*]
As much as an apple doth an oyster, and all one.

TRANIO [*as* LUCENTIO]
To save your life in this extremity
This favour will I do you for his sake;
And think it not the worst of all your fortunes
110   That you are like to Sir Vincentio.
His name and credit shall you undertake,
And in my house you shall be friendly lodg'd.

TRANIO, *as* LUCENTIO
It's death for anyone in Mantua
to come to Padua. Don't you know the reason?
Your ships are kept at Venice and the duke—
because of a private quarrel between your duke and him—
has decreed and publicly issued the order.   90
It's amazing you haven't heard, except that you just arrived.
Otherwise, you might have heard it proclaimed somewhere.

PEDANT
Alas, sir, it's even worse in my case
because I have bills for money from deals
in Florence and must deliver them here.   95

TRANIO, *as* LUCENTIO
Well, sir, to do you a favor
I'll do this and explain this to you—
but first, tell me, have you ever been in Pisa?

PEDANT
Yes, sir. I've often been in Pisa,
Pisa, famous for dignified citizens.   100

TRANIO, *as* LUCENTIO
Among those citizens, do you know one named Vincentio?

PEDANT
I don't personally know him, but I've heard of him.
He's a merchant of unmatched wealth.

TRANIO, *as* LUCENTIO
He's my father, sir. And to tell you the truth,
you somewhat resemble him in your bearing.   105

BIONDELLO (*aside*)
As much as an apple resembles an oyster, and that's beside
the point.

TRANIO, *as* LUCENTIO
To save your life when you're faced with this danger,
I'll do you a favor, for his sake—
and don't think it the worst of misfortunes
that you look like Sir Vincentio.   110
You'll assume his name and position
and be nicely settled in my house.

Look that you take upon you as you should;
You understand me, sir? So shall you stay
115 Till you have done your business in the city.
If this be court'sy, sir, accept of it.

PEDANT
O sir, I do, and will repute you ever
The patron of my life and liberty.

TRANIO [*as* LUCENTIO]
Then go with me to make the matter good.
120 This, by the way, I let you understand:
My father is here look'd for every day,
To pass assurance of a dow'r in marriage
'Twixt me and one Baptista's daughter here.
In all these circumstances I'll instruct you.
125 Go with me to clothe you as becomes you.

[*Exeunt.*]

Be sure you act your role as you should!
You get my meaning, sir? You can keep your part
until you've finished your business in the city.   115
If you take this to be a favor, sir, please accept my offer.

PEDANT

Oh sir, I do. And I'll esteem you forever
as the benefactor who gave me my life and freedom.

TRANIO, *as* LUCENTIO

Then come with me to settle the matter.
And I'll tell you this as we walk along: 120
my father is expected here any day now
to give guarantees on a marriage settlement
between myself and a daughter of a certain Baptista.
I'll tell you everything about the situation.
Come with me so that you can be dressed as is proper for you.   125

They exit.

ACT IV, SCENE III

[*A room in Petruchio's house.*] *Enter* KATHERINE *and* GRUMIO.

GRUMIO
No, no, forsooth, I dare not for my life.

KATHERINE
The more my wrong, the more his spite appears.
What, did he marry me to famish me?
Beggars, that come unto my father's door
5   Upon entreaty have a present alms.
If not, elsewhere they meet with charity.
But I, who never knew how to entreat,
Nor never needed that I should entreat,
Am starv'd for meat, giddy for lack of sleep,
10   With oaths kept waking, and with brawling fed.
And that which spites me more than all these wants,
He does it under name of perfect love,
As who should say, if I should sleep or eat
'Twere deadly sickness or else present death.
15   I prithee, go, and get me some repast;
I care not what, so it be wholesome food.

GRUMIO
What say you to a neat's foot?

KATHERINE
'Tis passing good; I prithee let me have it.

GRUMIO
I fear it is too choleric a meat.
20   How say you to a fat tripe finely broil'd?

KATHERINE
I like it well. Good Grumio, fetch it me.

GRUMIO
I cannot tell. I fear 'tis choleric.
What say you to a piece of beef and mustard?

ACT 4, SCENE 3

A room in PETRUCHIO'S *house.* KATHERINE *and*
GRUMIO *enter.*

GRUMIO
No, no, truly I can't, for fear of my life.

KATHERINE
The more he does to hurt me, the more malicious he becomes.
Really, did he marry me to starve me to death?
Beggars who come to my father's door
received some money immediately when they asked,   5
or if not, found charity elsewhere.
But I, who never learned to beg
and never needed to beg,
I am starved for food, dizzy from lack of sleep,
kept awake by swearing, and fed with fighting.   10
And the thing which irks me more than all the rest of my
    hungers
is that he does all this under the guise of the deepest love,
as if to say, if I should sleep or eat,
that would mean fatal sickness or even immediate death.
I beg you, go and get me some food.   15
I don't care what it is, just so long as it's nourishing.

GRUMIO
What do you say to a calf's foot?

KATHERINE
That would be wonderful. Please let me have it.

GRUMIO
I'm afraid it's a kind of meat that will make you hot-tempered.
What do you say to a fat tripe, broiled nicely?   20

KATHERINE
I'd like that very much. Grumio, go get it for me.

GRUMIO
I'm not sure; I'm afraid it might make you temperamental.
What do you say to a piece of beef with mustard?

KATHERINE

A dish that I do love to feed upon.

GRUMIO

25   Ay, but the mustard is too hot a little.

KATHERINE

Why then, the beef, and let the mustard rest.

GRUMIO

Nay then, I will not; you shall have the mustard,
Or else you get no beef of Grumio.

KATHERINE

Then both, or one, or any thing thou wilt.

GRUMIO

30   Why then, the mustard without the beef.

KATHERINE

Go, get thee gone, thou false deluding slave,

    [*Beats him.*]

That feed'st me with the very name of meat.
Sorrow on thee and all the pack of you,
That triumph thus upon my misery!
35   Go, get thee gone, I say.

       Enter PETRUCHIO *and* HORTENSIO *with meat.*

PETRUCHIO

How fares my Kate? What, sweeting, all amort!

HORTENSIO

Mistress, what cheer?

KATHERINE

              Faith, as cold as can be.

PETRUCHIO

Pluck up thy spirits; look cheerfully upon me.
40   Here, love, thou see'st how **diligent** I am,
To dress thy meat myself and bring it thee.
I am sure, sweet Kate, this kindness merits thanks.

KATHERINE

There's a dish I love to eat.

GRUMIO

Yes, but the mustard is a little too hot. 25

KATHERINE

Well then, just give me the beef and leave out the mustard.

GRUMIO

Oh no I won't. You'll take the mustard,
or else you won't get any beef from Grumio.

KATHERINE

Then give me both, or just one, or whatever you want.

GRUMIO

Well then, I'll give you the mustard without the beef. 30

KATHERINE

Go on, go away, you false, lying slave.

Beats him.

You feed me with just the name of food.
Bad luck to you and the whole lot of you
who delight in my misery!
Go, go away, I said. 35

PETRUCHIO *and* HORTENSIO *enter with food.*

PETRUCHIO

How are you doing, my Kate? What, my sweet? All down in the
mouth?

HORTENSIO

Mistress, how are you?

KATHERINE

Actually, I'm not feeling too well.

PETRUCHIO

Take heart. Give me a smile.
Here, love, you see how thoughtful I am 40
to prepare your food myself and bring it to you?
I'm sure, sweet Kate, that my thoughtfulness deserves a
thank-you.

What, not a word? Nay, then thou lov'st it not;
And all my pains is sorted to no proof.
45   Here, take away this dish.

KATHERINE
I pray you, let it stand.

PETRUCHIO
The poorest service is repaid with thanks,
And so shall mine, before you touch the meat.

KATHERINE
I thank you, sir.

HORTENSIO
50   Signior Petruchio, fie! You are to blame.
Come, Mistress Kate, I'll bear you company.

PETRUCHIO [*aside to* HORTENSIO]
Eat it up all, Hortensio, if thou lovest me.—
Much good do it unto thy gentle heart!
Kate, eat apace.

[KATHERINE *and* HORTENSIO *prepare to eat.*]

55   And now, my honey love,
Will we return unto thy father's house
And revel it as bravely as the best,
With silken coats and caps and golden rings,
With ruffs and cuffs and farthingales and things,
60   With scarves and fans and double change of brav'ry,
With amber bracelets, beads, and all this knav'ry.
What, hast thou din'd? The tailor stays thy leisure
To deck thy body with his ruffling treasure.

Enter TAILOR.

Come, tailor, let us see these ornaments;
65   Lay forth the gown.

Enter HABERDASHER. *

                    What news with you, sir?

HABERDASHER
Here is the cap your Worship did bespeak.

---

s.d.   *haberdasher* a hatmaker

What—not one word? Well, then, you must not like it,
and all my effort has been worthless.
Here, take this dish away.   45

KATHERINE
Please, leave it here!

PETRUCHIO
The most trifling favor is given thanks.
Mine will be, too, before you touch the food.

KATHERINE
I thank you, sir.

HORTENSIO
Signor Petruchio, for shame! You're the one to blame.   50
Come on, Mistress Kate, I'll keep you company.

PETRUCHIO (*aside*)
Eat it all up, Hortensio, if you want to please me.
I hope it does your gentle heart good!
(*To* KATE) Kate, dig in. And now, my sweet love,   55
we'll return to your father's house
and party in as fine clothing as the best of them,
with such coats and caps and golden rings,
with stiff collars, cuffs, hooped petticoats, and things,
with scarves, fans, and extra fancy clothing,   60
with amber bracelets, beads, and all sorts of trinkets.
What! Finished eating already? The tailor is waiting for you
    at your convenience
to cover you with his pretty ruffled treasures.

> TAILOR *enters.*

Come, tailor, let's see your pretty wares.
Lay out the gown.   65

> HABERDASHER *enters.*

What news do you bring, sir?

HABERDASHER
Here is the cap you ordered, your Worship.

PETRUCHIO

Why, this was moulded on a porringer;
A velvet dish. Fie, fie! 'Tis lewd and filthy.
70 Why, 'tis a cockle or a walnut shell,
A knack, a toy, a trick, a baby's cap.
Away with it! Come, let me have a bigger.

KATHERINE

I'll have no bigger; this doth fit the time,
And gentlewomen wear such caps as these.

PETRUCHIO

75 When you are gentle, you shall have one too,
And not till then.

HORTENSIO [*aside*]

That will not be in haste.

KATHERINE

Why, sir, I trust I may have leave to speak,
And speak I will. I am no child, no babe.
80 Your betters have endur'd me say my mind,
And if you cannot, best you stop your ears.
My tongue will tell the anger of my heart,
Or else my heart, concealing it, will break,
And rather than it shall, I will be free
85 Even to the uttermost, as I please, in words.

PETRUCHIO

Why, thou say'st true; it is a **paltry** cap,
A custard-coffin, a bauble, a silken pie.
I love thee well in that thou lik'st it not.

KATHERINE

Love me or love me not, I like the cap;
90 And it I will have, or I will have none.

[*Exit* HABERDASHER.]

PETRUCHIO

Thy gown? Why, ay. Come, tailor, let us see 't.
O mercy, God! What masquing stuff is here?

PETRUCHIO

Why, this was shaped on top of a soup bowl!
It's a velvet dish. For shame, for shame! This is repulsive and
    disgusting.
Why, it's a mollusk or a walnut shell, 70
a knickknack, a piece of fluff, a plaything, a baby's cap—
take it away! Come, bring me a bigger one.

KATHERINE

I don't want a bigger one. This one is fashionable,
and ladies wear caps like this.

PETRUCHIO

When you're a lady, you'll have one, too— 75
and not until then.

HORTENSIO (*aside*)

That won't be too soon.

KATHERINE

Why, sir, I trust that I have permission to speak,
and speak I will. I'm not a child or a baby.
Better people than you have listened to me speak my mind, 80
and if you can't, you'd better plug your ears.
I must voice my anger when I feel it,
or else break my heart concealing it.
Rather than do that, I'll speak freely,
even to an extreme, if I choose. 85

PETRUCHIO

Really, you're right. It's a shabby cap,
a custard cup, a bauble, a silken pie.
I love you for not liking it.

KATHERINE

Whether you love me or not, I like the cap,
and I'll have it or nothing. 90

      HABERDASHER *exits.*

PETRUCHIO

Your gown? Why, yes. Come, tailor, let's see it.
Oh my God! What kind of masquerade costume is that?

What's this? A sleeve? 'Tis like a demi-cannon.*
What, up and down, carv'd like an apple-tart?
95 Here's snip and nip and cut and slish and slash,
Like to a censer in a barber's shop.
Why, what i' devil's name, tailor, call'st thou this?

HORTENSIO [aside]
I see she's like to have neither cap nor gown.

TAILOR
You bid me make it orderly and well,
100 According to the fashion and the time.

PETRUCHIO
Marry, and did. But if you be rememb'red,
I did not bid you mar it to the time.
Go, hop me over every kennel home,
For you shall hop without my custom, sir.
105 I'll none of it. Hence, make your best of it!

KATHERINE
I never saw a better-fashion'd gown,
More quaint, more pleasing, nor more commendable.
Belike you mean to make a puppet of me.

PETRUCHIO
Why, true, he means to make a puppet of thee.

TAILOR
110 She says your Worship means to make a puppet of her.

PETRUCHIO
O monstrous arrogance! Thou liest, thou thread, thou
    thimble,
Thou yard, three-quarters, half-yard, quarter, nail!
Thou flea, thou nit, thou winter cricket thou!
115 Brav'd in mine own house with a skein of thread?
Away, thou rag, thou quantity, thou remnant,
Or I shall so be-mete* thee with thy yard
As thou shalt think on prating whilst thou liv'st!
I tell thee, I, that thou hast marr'd her gown.

---

93 *demi-cannon* a large cannon and a type of sleeve that was tapered from the
shoulder to the waist

117 *be-mete* means both "measure" and "beat"

What's this—a sleeve? It's like a big cannon.
What! Carved everywhere like an apple tart?
Here's a snip, there a nip, a cut, a slish, a slash— 95
like an incense burner in a barber's shop.
Why, what in the devil do you call this, tailor?

HORTENSIO (*aside*)
I see she's not likely to get either a cap or a gown.

TAILOR
You told me to make it neatly and well,
according to what is fashionable and in style. 100

PETRUCHIO
Indeed, I did. But if you recall,
I did not tell you to ruin it for all time.
Go and jump over every gutter on your way home,
for you'll have to get along without my business, sir.
I won't have any of this. Go away. Take this as you please. 105

KATHERINE
I never saw a better-made dress,
more elegant, more pleasing, or more commendable.
You probably want to make me a puppet.

PETRUCHIO
Why, that's the truth—he wants to make you a puppet.

TAILOR
She said you, your Worship, wanted to make a puppet of her. 110

PETRUCHIO
Oh you monstrously arrogant man! You're lying, you thread,
    you thimble,
you yard, three-quarters, half-, quarter-, sixteenth of a yard!
You flea, you louse egg, you winter cricket, you!
Defied in my own house by a coil of thread! 115
Go away you rag, you fragment, you scrap,
or I'll beat you so badly with your yardstick
that you'll never forget your stupid remark while you live!
I'm telling you, you ruined her dress.

TAILOR

120 Your Worship is deceiv'd; the gown is made
Just as my master had direction.
Grumio gave order how it should be done.

GRUMIO

I gave him no order; I gave him the stuff.

TAILOR

But how did you desire it should be made?

GRUMIO

125 Marry, sir, with needle and thread.

TAILOR

But did you not request to have it cut?

GRUMIO

Thou hast fac'd* many things.

TAILOR

I have.

GRUMIO

Face not me; thou hast brav'd* many men, brave not me; I
130 will neither be fac'd nor brav'd. I say unto thee, I bid thy
master cut out the gown; but I did not bid him cut it to
pieces; *ergo,* thou liest.

TAILOR

Why, here is the note of the fashion to testify.

[*He shows a paper.*]

PETRUCHIO

Read it.

GRUMIO

135 The note lies in 's throat, if he say I said so.

TAILOR [*Reads.*]

"*Imprimis,* a loose-bodied gown"—*

---

127 *fac'd* means both "defiantly opposed" and "trimmed"

129 *brav'd* means both "defied" and "elegantly made"

136 *loose-bodied gown* a dress for home wear. But "loose" also implies that the dress is
for a prostitute.

TAILOR
You're mistaken, your Worship. The dress was made   120
just as you told my master to make it.
Grumio gave me orders how to do it.

GRUMIO
I didn't give him any orders; I just gave him the stuff to make it.

TAILOR
But how did you want it made?

GRUMIO
Indeed, sir, with a needle and thread.   125

TAILOR
But didn't you ask for me to cut it?

GRUMIO
You've cut lots of clothes.

TAILOR
Yes, I have.

GRUMIO
Well, don't cut me. You've dressed many men in fancy clothes;
don't defy me. I won't be cut or defied. I tell you, I told your   130
master to cut out the gown, but I did not tell him to cut it to
pieces. Therefore, you're lying.

TAILOR
Why, here's a written order for the dress design to back me up.

Shows a paper.

PETRUCHIO
Read it.

GRUMIO
The note is a calculating liar if it says I said so.   135

TAILOR (*Reads.*)
"First, a loose-fitting dress."

GRUMIO

Master, if ever I said "loose-bodied gown," sew me in the skirts of it and beat me to death with a bottom of brown thread. I said "a gown."

PETRUCHIO

140 Proceed.

TAILOR [*Reads.*]

"With a small compass'd cape"—

GRUMIO

I confess the cape.

TAILOR [*Reads.*]

"With a trunk sleeve"—

GRUMIO

I confess two sleeves.

TAILOR [*Reads.*]

145 "The sleeves curiously cut."

PETRUCHIO

Ay, there's the villainy.

GRUMIO

Error i' th' bill, sir, error i' th' bill.* I commanded the sleeves should be cut out and sew'd up again, and that I'll prove upon thee, though thy little finger be armed in
150 a thimble.

TAILOR

This is true that I say. An I had thee in place where, thou shouldst know it.

GRUMIO

I am for thee straight. Take thou the bill, give me thy mete-yard, and spare not me.

HORTENSIO

155 God-a-mercy, Grumio, then he shall have no odds!

PETRUCHIO

Well, sir, in brief, the gown is not for me.

---

147 *bill* means both "a written order" and a kind of weapon

GRUMIO

Master, if I ever said a "loose-fitting dress," sew me up in the skirts of it, and beat me to death with a spool of brown thread. I said "a gown."

PETRUCHIO

Go on. 140

TAILOR (*Reads.*)

"With a small, circular cape."

GRUMIO

I agree that's what I said about the cape.

TAILOR (*Reads.*)

"With a full sleeve."

GRUMIO

I admit to ordering two sleeves.

TAILOR (*Reads.*)

"The sleeves cut with fine details." 145

PETRUCHIO

Yes, there's the villainy.

GRUMIO

Error in the note, sir; error in the note! I ordered that the sleeves should be cut out and sewed up again, and I'll fight you to prove it, even if your little finger is armored in a thimble. 150

TAILOR

What I told you was the truth—and if we were in the right place, you'd find that out.

GRUMIO

I'm ready for you right now. You take the note and give me your yardstick and don't pull any punches.

HORTENSIO

Heavens, Grumio! Then he won't have a chance. 155

PETRUCHIO

Well, sir, in short: I don't think the dress suits me.

GRUMIO

You are i' th' right, sir, 'tis for my mistress.

PETRUCHIO

Go, take it up unto thy master's use.

GRUMIO

Villain, not for thy life! Take up my mistress's gown for
thy master's use!*

PETRUCHIO

Why, sir, what's your conceit in that?

GRUMIO

O, sir, the conceit is deeper than you think for. Take up
my mistress's gown to his master's use! O, fie, fie, fie!

PETRUCHIO [*aside*]

Hortensio, say thou wilt see the tailor paid. [*to* TAILOR]
Go take it hence. Begone, and say no more.

HORTENSIO [*aside*]

Tailor, I'll pay thee for thy gown tomorrow;
Take no unkindness of his hasty words.
Away, I say. Commend me to thy master.

[*Exit* TAILOR.]

PETRUCHIO

Well, come, my Kate, we will unto your father's
Even in these honest mean habiliments.
Our purses shall be proud, our garments poor,
For 'tis the mind that makes the body rich,
And as the sun breaks through the darkest clouds,
So honour peereth in the meanest habit.
What, is the jay more precious than the lark
Because his feathers are more beautiful?
Or is the adder better than the eel,
Because his painted skin contents the eye?
O, no, good Kate; neither art thou the worse
For this poor furniture and mean array.
If thou account'st it shame, lay it on me,
And therefore frolic. We will hence forthwith

---

160 *use* Grumio plays on the meaning of use "to have sex with"

GRUMIO
You're right there, sir; it's for my lady.

PETRUCHIO
Go and pick it up for your master to use however he can.

GRUMIO
Don't you dare, you rascal! Pick up my lady's dress for my
master to use?   160

PETRUCHIO
What notion is bothering you, sir?

GRUMIO
Oh, sir, the meaning is deeper than you think.
To pick up my lady's gown so his master can use her as he likes?
Oh shame, shame, shame!

PETRUCHIO (*to* HORTENSIO *privately*)
Hortensio, see that the tailor is paid. (to TAILOR)
Go, and take the dress. Go, and not another word.   165

HORTENSIO (*privately to* TAILOR)
Tailor, I'll pay you for the dress tomorrow.
Don't resent his hot-tempered words.
Go, I said! Say hello to your master for me.

           TAILOR *exits.*

PETRUCHIO
Well, come, my Kate. We'll go to your father's
just in these decent, simple clothes.   170
Our purses will be rich if our clothes are poor
because it's the mind that makes the body rich.
And just as the sun breaks through the darkest clouds,
so honor shines through the crudest clothing.
Why, is the jay more treasured than the lark   175
because his feathers are more beautiful?
Or is the adder better than the eel
because his colorful skin is nice to look at?
No, good Kate. And neither are you any the worse
for your simple outfit and cheap dress.   180
If you are embarrassed, blame it on me.
So, be happy. We'll leave here at once

To feast and sport us at thy father's house.—
Go, call my men, and let us straight to him,
185 And bring our horses unto Long-lane end.
There will we mount, and thither walk on foot.
Let's see, I think 'tis now some seven o'clock,
And well we may come there by dinner time.

KATHERINE
I dare assure you, sir, 'tis almost two,
190 And 'twill be supper time ere you come there.

PETRUCHIO
It shall be seven ere I go to horse.
Look, what I speak, or do, or think to do,
You are still crossing it. Sirs, let 't alone,
I will not go today, and ere I do,
195 It shall be what o'clock I say it is.

HORTENSIO [*aside*]
Why, so, this gallant will command the sun.

[*Exeunt.*]

to feast and enjoy ourselves at your father's house.
(*To* GRUMIO) Go call my men, and let's set out for his house
   right now.
Bring our horses to the end of Long Lane—   185
we'll walk there and mount at that point.
Let's see, I think it's now about seven o'clock,
and we'll probably be there about noon.

KATHERINE

   I assure you, sir, it's almost two,
   and it will be suppertime before we reach my father's house.   190

PETRUCHIO

   It will be seven before we leave.
   Whatever I say or do or plan to do,
   you always contradict me. Gentlemen, forget it.
   I'm not leaving today. And before I do,
   it will be the time I say it is.   195

HORTENSIO (*aside*)

   Why, this lordly man will give the sun orders!

    They exit.

ACT IV, SCENE IV

[*Padua. Before Baptista's house.*] *Enter* TRANIO [*as* LUCENTIO], *and the* PEDANT *dressed like* VINCENTIO.

TRANIO [*as* LUCENTIO]
Sir, this is the house; please it you that I call?

PEDANT
Ay, what else? And but I be deceived,
Signior Baptista may remember me,
Near twenty years ago, in Genoa,

5 Where we were lodgers at the Pegasus.*

TRANIO [*as* LUCENTIO]
'Tis well; and hold your own, in any case,
With such **austerity** as 'longeth to a father.

PEDANT
I warrant you.

Enter BIONDELLO.

But, sir, here comes your boy;
10 'Twere good he were school'd.

TRANIO [*as* LUCENTIO]
Fear you not him.—Sirrah Biondello,
Now do your duty throughly, I advise you.
Imagine 'twere the right Vincentio.

BIONDELLO
Tut, fear not me.

TRANIO [*as* LUCENTIO]
15 But hast thou done thy errand to Baptista?

BIONDELLO
I told him that your father was at Venice,
And that you look'd for him this day in Padua.

TRANIO [*as* LUCENTIO]
Thou'rt a tall fellow. Hold thee that to drink.

[*He gives him money.*]

---

5 *Pegasus* a common name for an inn

ACT 4, SCENE 4

Padua. Before BAPTISTA'S *house.* TRANIO (*as* LUCENTIO) *and the* PEDANT, *dressed like* VINCENTIO, *enter.*

TRANIO, *as* LUCENTIO
Sir, this is the house. Should I stop and knock?

PEDANT
Certainly, why not? Unless I miss my guess,
Signor Baptista may remember me
from about twenty years ago in Genoa,
when we both stayed at the Pegasus.   5

TRANIO, *as* LUCENTIO
That's well-acted. And play your part, doing everything
with the dignity of a father.

PEDANT
I promise you, I will. But sir, here comes your young servant—
you'd better let him in on the secret.   10

> BIONDELLO *enters.*

TRANIO, *as* LUCENTIO
Don't worry about him. My servant, Biondello,
do your duty thoroughly now, I warn you.
You must imagine he's the real Vincentio.

BIONDELLO
Nonsense, don't worry about me.

TRANIO, *as* LUCENTIO
But have you run your errand to Baptista?   15

BIONDELLO
I told him that your father was in Venice
and that you expected him in Padua today.

TRANIO, *as* LUCENTIO
You're a wonderful fellow—save this for a drink.

> *Gives him a coin.*

Enter BAPTISTA *and* LUCENTIO [*as* CAMBIO].
PEDANT *booted and bareheaded.*

Here comes Baptista; set your countenance, sir.

20 Signior Baptista, you are happily met.—
[*to the* PEDANT]. Sir, this is the gentleman I told you of.
I pray you, stand good father to me now.
Give me Bianca for my patrimony.

PEDANT [*as* VINCENTIO]
Soft, son!—

25 Sir, by your leave, having come to Padua
To gather in some debts, my son Lucentio
Made me acquainted with a weighty cause
Of love between your daughter and himself.
And, for the good report I hear of you,

30 And for the love he beareth to your daughter
And she to him, to stay him not too long,
I am content, in a good father's care,
To have him match'd. And if you please to like
No worse than I, upon some agreement

35 Me shall you find ready and willing
With one consent to have her so bestow'd,
For curious I cannot be with you,
Signior Baptista, of whom I hear so well.

BAPTISTA
Sir, pardon me in what I have to say.

40 Your plainness and your shortness please me well.
Right true it is, your son Lucentio here
Doth love my daughter and she loveth him,
Or both **dissemble** deeply their affections.
And therefore, if you say no more than this,

45 That like a father you will deal with him
And pass my daughter a sufficient dower,
The match is made, and all is done.
Your son shall have my daughter with consent.

BAPTISTA *and* LUCENTIO (*as* CAMBIO) *enter.* PEDANT *is wearing boots and not wearing a hat.*

Here comes Baptista. Assume your proper style, sir.
Signor Baptista, this is a fortunate meeting. 20
(*to the* PEDANT) Sir, this is the gentleman I told you about.
I ask you to act like a good father to me now.
Give me Bianca for my patrimony.

PEDANT (*as* VINCENTIO)
Slow down, son!—
Sir, if you'll permit me to explain—having come to Padua 25
to collect some debts, my son Lucentio
told me about a serious case
of love between your daughter and himself.
And because of your good reputation
and his love for your daughter 30
and her love for him, I won't delay him too long.
I'm satisfied, like any good father,
to have him married. And if you're content to favor the marriage
as much as I am, then—after a marriage settlement has been
    made—
you'll find me ready and willing, 35
and with my hearty approval, to agree to her marriage to him.
For I can't be picky about the little details with you,
Signor Baptista, of whom I've heard so many good things.

BAPTISTA
Sir, please excuse me for what I'm going to say.
Your frankness and conciseness please me a great deal. 40
It's certainly true that your son Lucentio, here,
loves my daughter and that she loves him—
or they're both wonderful pretenders.
So, if you promise just this,
that you'll treat him like a father 45
and guarantee my daughter a sufficient marriage settlement,
I'll agree to the marriage, and it will be settled.
Your son will have my daughter with my blessings.

TRANIO [*as* LUCENTIO]
  I thank you, sir. Where, then, do you know best
50 We be affied and such assurance ta'en
  As shall with either part's agreement stand?

BAPTISTA
  Not in my house, Lucentio, for you know,
  Pitchers have ears, and I have many servants.
  Besides, old Gremio is heark'ning still,
55 And haply we might be interrupted.

TRANIO [*as* LUCENTIO]
  Then at my lodging, an it like you.
  There doth my father lie, and there this night
  We'll pass the business privately and well.
  Send for your daughter by your servant here.

    [*He indicates* LUCENTIO, *with a wink.*]

60 My boy shall fetch the scrivener presently.
  The worst is this, that, at so slender warning
  You are like to have a thin and slender pittance.

BAPTISTA
  It likes me well.—Cambio, hie you home,
  And bid Bianca make her ready straight.
65 And, if you will, tell what hath happened:
  Lucentio's father is arriv'd in Padua,
  And how she's like to be Lucentio's wife.

    [*Exit* LUCENTIO.]

BIONDELLO
  I pray the gods she may with all my heart!

TRANIO [*as* LUCENTIO]
  Dally not with the gods, but get thee gone.—
70 Signior Baptista, shall I lead the way?
  Welcome! One mess is like to be your cheer;
  Come, sir, we will better it in Pisa.

TRANIO (*as* LUCENTIO)
I thank you, sir. Where, then, do you think it's best
that we be formally engaged and give pledges   50
that will suit both parties?

BAPTISTA
Not in my house, Lucentio. You know
that pitchers have ears, and I have many servants.
Besides, old Gremio is always eavesdropping,
and perhaps we might be interrupted.   55

TRANIO (*as* LUCENTIO)
Then we'll do it at my house, if you like.
That's where my father is staying, and there, tonight,
we'll settle the business secretly and satisfactorily.
Send your servant here to get your daughter.

He indicates LUCENTIO *and winks at him.*

My servant will fetch the notary immediately.   60
The worst you can expect is this: that at such short notice,
you're likely to get a scanty, light meal.

BAPTISTA
That suits me well.—Cambio, hurry home
and tell Bianca to get ready right away.
And if you will, tell her what has happened—   65
that Lucentio's father has arrived in Padua
and that she's likely to become Lucentio's wife.

LUCENTIO *exits.*

BIONDELLO
I pray to the gods with all my heart that she may!

TRANIO (*as* LUCENTIO)
Don't waste time with the gods, but get going.—
Signor Baptista, shall I lead the way?   70
You are welcome, though one course is likely to be all the
    meal you'll get.
Come, sir, we'll do better for you in Pisa.

BAPTISTA
I follow you.

[*All but* BIONDELLO *exit.*]

Reenter LUCENTIO *and* BIONDELLO.

BIONDELLO
Cambio!

LUCENTIO
75   What say'st thou, Biondello?

BIONDELLO
You saw my master wink and laugh upon you?

LUCENTIO
Biondello, what of that?

BIONDELLO
Faith, nothing; but has left me here behind to **expound**
the meaning or moral of his signs and tokens.

LUCENTIO
80   I pray thee, moralize them.

BIONDELLO
Then thus: Baptista is safe, talking with the deceiving
father of a deceitful son.

LUCENTIO
And what of him?

BIONDELLO
His daughter is to be brought by you to the supper.

LUCENTIO
85   And then?

BIONDELLO
The old priest of Saint Luke's church is at your command
at all hours.

LUCENTIO
And what of all this?

BIONDELLO
I cannot tell. Except they are busied about a counterfeit
90   assurance. Take you assurance of her, *cum privilegio ad*

BAPTISTA
I'll follow you.

All but BIONDELLO *exit.*

LUCENTIO *and* BIONDELLO *enter.*

BIONDELLO
Cambio!

LUCENTIO
What did you want to say, Biondello? 75

BIONDELLO
You saw my "master" wink and laugh at you?

LUCENTIO
So what, Biondello?

BIONDELLO
Really, nothing—except that he has left me behind here to explain the meaning or significance of his signs and hints.

LUCENTIO
Please explain them. 80

BIONDELLO
It's like this. Baptista is taken care of, talking with the fake father of a fake son.

LUCENTIO
And what about him?

BIONDELLO
You're supposed to take his daughter to their supper.

LUCENTIO
And then? 85

BIONDELLO
The old priest at Saint Luke's church is ready and waiting for you at any time.

LUCENTIO
So what about all this?

BIONDELLO
I don't know—except that while they're busy with a fake marriage settlement, you should settle with her on the 90

imprimendum solum. * To th' church. Take the priest, clerk,
and some sufficient honest witnesses.
If this be not that you look for, I have no more to say,
But bid Bianca farewell forever and a day.

LUCENTIO

95   Hear'st thou, Biondello?

BIONDELLO

I cannot tarry. I knew a wench married in an afternoon as
she went to the garden for parsley to stuff a rabbit, and so
may you, sir. And so, adieu, sir. My master hath appointed
me to go to Saint Luke's to bid the priest be ready to come
100   against you come with your appendix.

    [Exit.]

LUCENTIO

I may, and will, if she be so contented.
She will be pleased; then wherefore should I doubt?
Hap what hap may, I'll roundly go about her;
It shall go hard if "Cambio" go without her.

    [Exit.]

90–91   *cum privilegio ad imprimendum solum*   a phrase giving a printer the sole rights to
print

exclusive right of printing. Go to the church! Get the priest, a clerk, and enough honest witnesses. If this isn't the chance that you were looking for, I'll shut up. But you might as well say good-bye to Bianca for forever.

LUCENTIO

Do you hear yourself, Biondello? 95

BIONDELLO

I can't stay any longer. I knew a woman married in an afternoon as she went to the garden to get parsley for stuffing for a rabbit. You could, too, sir. So, good-bye, sir. My "master" has ordered me to go to Saint Luke's to tell the priest to be prepared for you when you come with your wife. 100

Exit.

LUCENTIO

I may and will do that, if she is willing.
She will be pleased—so what am I doubting about?
Let what happens, happen. I'll go after her right now.
Only a disaster can keep "Cambio" from marrying her now.

Exit.

ACT IV, SCENE V

[*A public road.*] *Enter* PETRUCHIO, KATHERINE, HORTENSIO, *and* SERVANTS.

PETRUCHIO
Come on, i' God's name, once more toward our father's.
Good Lord, how bright and goodly shines the moon!

KATHERINE
The moon? The sun! It is not moonlight now.

PETRUCHIO
I say it is the moon that shines so bright.

KATHERINE
5   I know it is the sun that shines so bright.

PETRUCHIO
Now, by my mother's son, and that's myself,
It shall be moon, or star, or what I list,
Or ere I journey to your father's house. [*to* SERVANTS]
Go on, and fetch our horses back again.—
10   Evermore cross'd and cross'd, nothing but cross'd!

HORTENSIO [*to* KATHERINE]
Say as he says, or we shall never go.

KATHERINE
Forward, I pray, since we have come so far,
And be it moon, or sun, or what you please.
An if you please to call it a rush candle,*
15   Henceforth I vow it shall be so for me.

PETRUCHIO
I say it is the moon.

KATHERINE
I know it is the moon.

PETRUCHIO
Nay, then you lie; it is the blessed sun.

---

14   *rush candle* a candle made from a rush, coated with grease

ACT 4, SCENE 5

A public road. PETRUCHIO, KATE, HORTENSIO, *and*
SERVANTS *enter.*

PETRUCHIO
Come on, in God's name. Let's go once more to my
father-in-law's.
Good Lord, how bright and well the moon is shining!

KATHERINE
The moon! You mean the sun; the moon isn't out now.

PETRUCHIO
I say it's the moon that's shining so brightly.

KATHERINE
I know it's the sun that's shining so brightly.   5

PETRUCHIO
Now, by my mother's son, and that means me,
it will be the moon, or a star, or whatever I please
before we go back to your father's house.
(*to* SERVANTS) Go and bring our horses back again.
I'm constantly contradicted and contradicted; nothing but
contradicted.   10

HORTENSIO (*to* KATHERINE)
Say what he says or we'll never get moving.

KATHERINE
Please, let's go on since we've come so far,
and let it be the moon or sun or whatever you want.
If you want to call it a rush candle,
I swear that from now on I'll call it that.   15

PETRUCHIO
I say it is the moon.

KATHERINE
I know it is the moon.

PETRUCHIO
Well then, you're lying; it's the blessed sun.

KATHERINE

Then, God be bless'd, it is the blessed sun.

20 But sun it is not, when you say it is not,
And the moon changes even as your mind.
What you will have it nam'd, even that it is,
And so it shall be so for Katherine.

HORTENSIO

Petruchio, go thy ways, the field is won.

PETRUCHIO

25 Well, forward, forward. Thus the bowl should run,
And not unluckily against the bias.*
But, soft! Company is coming here.

     Enter VINCENTIO.

[*to* VINCENTIO] Good morrow, gentle mistress; where
    away?—
30 Tell me, sweet Kate, and tell me truly too,
Hast thou beheld a fresher gentlewoman?
Such war of white and red within her cheeks!
What stars do spangle heaven with such beauty
As those two eyes become that heavenly face?—
35 Fair lovely maid, once more good day to thee.—
Sweet Kate, embrace her for her beauty's sake.

HORTENSIO [*aside*]

'A will make the man mad, to make the woman of him.

KATHERINE

Young budding virgin, fair and fresh and sweet,
Whither away, or where is thy abode?
40 Happy the parents of so fair a child!
Happier the man, whom favourable stars
Allots thee for his lovely bedfellow!

PETRUCHIO

Why, how now, Kate! I hope thou art not mad.
This is a man—old, wrinkled, faded, withered—
45 And not a maiden, as thou say'st he is.

---

26 *bias* lead in the side of a bowling ball that causes the ball to swerve when
bowled properly

KATHERINE

Then, bless God, it's the blessed sun!
But it's not the sun when you say it isn't, 20
and the moon changes when you change your mind.
Whatever you want it to be called, it will be called exactly that,
and Kate will accept whatever you say.

HORTENSIO

Petruchio, go on; you've won the fight.

PETRUCHIO

Well, let's go, let's go! The bowling ball should roll like this 25
and not unluckily with a bad curve.
But wait a minute! Someone is approaching.

     VINCENTIO *enters.*

(*to* VINCENTIO) Good day, gentle lady; where are you going?—
Tell me, sweet Kate, and tell me the truth, too, 30
have you ever seen a more glowing gentlewoman?
Such a mix of white and red on her cheeks!
What stars sparkle in the heaven with the beauty
that those two eyes shine in her heavenly face?—
Pretty, lovely lady, I say good day to you once again.— 35
Sweet Kate, give her a hug for the sake of her beauty.

HORTENSIO (*aside*)

He will make the man mad if he tries to make a woman out of
   him.

KATHERINE

Young, blooming virgin, pretty and fresh and sweet,
where are you going, or where do you live?
The parents of such a pretty child must feel lucky. 40
The man whom good fortune lets have
you for his lovely mate will be even luckier.

PETRUCHIO

Why, what's wrong, Kate! I hope you're not crazy.
This is a man—old, wrinkled, faded, and withered—
and not a girl, as you said he was. 45

KATHERINE

Pardon, old father, my mistaking eyes,
That have been so bedazzled with the sun
That everything I look on seemeth green.
Now I perceive thou art a reverend father.
50 Pardon, I pray thee, for my mad mistaking.

PETRUCHIO

Do, good old grandsire, and withal make known
Which way thou travellest. If along with us,
We shall be joyful of thy company.

VINCENTIO

Fair sir, and you, my merry mistress,
55 That with your strange encounter much amaz'd me,
My name is call'd Vincentio, my dwelling Pisa,
And bound I am to Padua, there to visit
A son of mine, which long I have not seen.

PETRUCHIO

What is his name?

VINCENTIO

60   Lucentio, gentle sir.

PETRUCHIO

Happily met, the happier for thy son.
And now by law, as well as reverend age,
I may entitle thee my loving father.
The sister to my wife, this gentlewoman,
65 Thy son by this hath married. Wonder not,
Nor be not griev'd. She is of good esteem,
Her dowry wealthy, and of worthy birth;
Beside, so qualified as may beseem
The spouse of any noble gentleman.
70 Let me embrace with old Vincentio,
And wander we to see thy honest son,
Who will of thy arrival be full joyous.

VINCENTIO

But is this true, or is it else your pleasure,
Like pleasant travelers, to break a jest
75 Upon the company you overtake?

KATHERINE

Forgive me, old sir. My mistaken eyes
have been so dazzled by the sun
that everything I look at seems young.
Now I see that you are a venerable gentleman.
Please forgive me for my crazy mistake.   50

PETRUCHIO

Please do, good old gentleman. And now, tell us
which way you're traveling. If you're going our way,
we'd be happy to have your company.

VINCENTIO

Good sir, and you, my merry lady—
who shocked me so much by your strange greeting—   55
my name is Vincentio. I live in Pisa.
And I'm headed for Padua to visit
a son of mine there, whom I haven't seen in a long time.

PETRUCHIO

What's his name?

VINCENTIO

Lucentio, good sir.   60

PETRUCHIO

This is a fortunate meeting—the more fortunate for your son.
And now legally, as well as out of respect to your dignified age,
I may call you my loving father.
The sister to my wife—this lady here—
has married your son by now. Don't be astonished   65
or sad. She is well-respected,
her dowry is big, and she's from a good family.
Besides that, she has qualities that are proper
for the wife of any noble gentleman.
Let me hug you, old Vincentio,   70
and let's go to see your honest son,
who will be delighted by your arrival.

VINCENTIO

Is this true? Or else is it your idea of fun,
like merry travelers, to pull a trick
on the people you overtake?   75

HORTENSIO

I do assure thee, father, so it is.

PETRUCHIO

Come, go along and see the truth hereof,
For our first merriment hath made thee jealous.

[*Exeunt all but* HORTENSIO.]

HORTENSIO

Well, Petruchio, this has put me in heart.
80 Have to my widow, and if she be froward,
Then hast thou taught Hortensio to be untoward.

[*Exit.*]

HORTENSIO

I assure you, father, it's as he said.

PETRUCHIO

Come, go along with us, and see that it's true,
since our first jokes made you suspicious.

All but HORTENSIO *exit.*

HORTENSIO

Well, Petruchio, this has made me jealous.
Onward to my widow! And if she's stubborn,   80
then you've taught Hortensio how to get his way.

Exit.

Act IV Review

Discussion Questions

1. What elements of farce are present in Grumio and Curtis's encounter?

2. How do you know that Kate has changed, both from Grumio's account and by her own behavior when she enters Petruchio's country home?

3. How does Bianca and Lucentio's exchange in Scene ii compare to their last meeting?

4. What is ironic about Hortensio's resolution to seek kindness in a woman and not beauty?

5. How does the recruitment of the Pedant further the theme of deception?

6. What new awareness on Kate's part is revealed by her conversation with Grumio?

7. What is revealed by Kate's outburst at Petruchio over the cap and gown?

8. What do Petruchio's tests of Kate in Scene v prove?

Literary Elements

1. **Metaphors** make a direct comparison between unlike things. Find any metaphors in Act IV and explain how the comparisons contribute to the play.

2. **An extended metaphor** makes a point-by-point comparison of two unlike things. Look at the extended metaphor Petruchio draws in Act IV, Scene i, lines 171–192. Decide what the comparison is and explain the various points of comparison.

3. Good drama has **conflict**: struggle between opposing forces. In Act IV, Shakespeare heightens the conflict between Petruchio and Kate. Find examples of how Petruchio's behavior increases the conflict. Then, explain how Kate's actions are affected. Are these two people well-matched?

4. A **soliloquy** expresses a character's private thoughts, even if other characters are on stage. At the end of Act IV, Scene i, Petruchio delivers a soliloquy that compares taming a falcon to taming a wife. As you read it, see if you can find any true expression of love for Kate in his words.

Writing Prompts

1. Write a soliloquy in Elizabethan language giving Kate's reaction to Petruchio's treatment of her after their wedding.

2. What factor is most responsible for the difficulties facing Petruchio and Kate as a couple? Write an essay that explains your opinion, supporting it with examples from the play.

3. In the language of Shakespeare's day, write a letter to Bianca from Lucentio proposing that the two elope.

4. Pretend that women had the upper hand in Shakespeare's day. Write a series of tests that Kate could give to Petruchio to tame *him*.

5. Write an opinion essay on the theme of deception and hypocrisy, one that incorporates one or more quotations or short summaries from the events in *The Taming of the Shrew*.

The Taming of the Shrew

ACT V

Raul Julia as Petruchio with a submissive Kate, Meryl Streep, Delacorte Theatre, 1978

"Thou hast tam'd a curst shrew."

Before You Read

1. Consider all the ways in which Petruchio and Kate are a match for each other.

2. How well do you think Lucentio and Hortensio really know their new wives?

3. Shakespeare's comedies typically end with a wedding feast. What does such a convention achieve?

Literary Elements

1. **Irony** refers to the distance between reality and appearance. In Act IV, it is ironic that Petruchio tortures Kate by denying her food, sleep, and other essentials while pretending to be a model new husband.

2. **Imagery** refers to vivid, descriptive language that refers to the five senses (taste, touch, hearing, smell, or sight). There are many images of animals in *The Taming of the Shrew*, often made in reference to Kate or the other women of the play. In Act II, Baptista says to Kate, "For shame, thou hilding [beast] of a devilish spirit!"

3. A **theme** is the underlying meaning or message of a work of literature. Shakespeare explores many themes in *The Taming of the Shrew*, including the obstacles to young love.

4. As you learned earlier in Act IV, a **symbol** is a person, place, object, or action that represents a more abstract concept. Baptista's award of Bianca's hand to the highest bidder—Lucentio—symbolizes the fact that in Elizabethan times, marriages were often economic transactions.

Words to Know

The following vocabulary words appear in Act V in the original text of Shakespeare's play. However, they are words that are still used today. Read the definitions here and pay attention to the words as you read the play (they will be in boldfaced type).

bandy	exchange; toss around
bereft	without; deprived of
bodes	foreshadow; hints at
confounds	confuse; bewilder
controversy	argument; dispute
dotard	a senile person
frivolous	trivial; insignificant
galled [gall'd]	annoyed; angered
notorious	infamous; dishonorable
peevish	irritable; bad-tempered

Act Summary

Bianca and Lucentio marry. The real Vincentio arrives at Lucentio's house, where the Pedant is pretending to be him. Vincentio is at the point of being arrested when Bianca and Lucentio come back from getting married and Lucentio explains what has happened. At first Baptista is angry, but Vincentio assures him that he will bless the marriage of Lucentio and Bianca. Petruchio begs a kiss of Kate but she refuses at first, not wanting to do so in public. He threatens to return home, so she kisses him after all. They go inside with the others.

Everyone gathers at the marriage feast of Lucentio to Bianca, Hortensio to the Widow, and now Petruchio to Kate. The Widow has a spiteful disagreement with Kate, and all of the women withdraw. For fun, the men make a wager: They will test their wives to see which is most obedient. First Bianca is sent for, but she refuses to come. Next, the Widow refuses to return to the wedding feast. At Petruchio's request, however, Kate returns immediately.

Bianca lets Lucentio know he is a fool for betting on her own obedience. At Petruchio's urging, Kate lectures the women present on the virtues of submitting to their husbands' authority. She claims that women owe their husbands the same allegiance that citizens of the Crown owe their prince. Her own rebellion gained her nothing. Petruchio seems to revel in her new attitude, and after getting a kiss from her, takes her home to bed. The others are astounded by his success at taming such a shrew.

Elizabeth Taylor and Richard Burton in Zeffirelli film, 1967

ACT V, SCENE I

[*Padua. Before Lucentio's house.*] *Enter* BIONDELLO,
LUCENTIO [*as himself*], *and* BIANCA. GREMIO *is
out before* [*and stands to the side*].

BIONDELLO
Softly and swiftly, sir, for the priest is ready.

LUCENTIO
I fly, Biondello; but they may chance to need thee at
home. Therefore leave us.

[*Exit* LUCENTIO *and* BIANCA.]

BIONDELLO
Nay, faith, I'll see the church a' your back, and then come
5   back to my master's as soon as I can.

[*Exit.*]

GREMIO
I marvel Cambio comes not all this while.

Enter PETRUCHIO, KATHERINE, VINCENTIO,
GRUMIO, *with* ATTENDANTS.

PETRUCHIO
Sir, here's the door, this is Lucentio's house.
My father's bears more toward the marketplace.
Thither must I, and here I leave you, sir.

VINCENTIO
10   You shall not choose but drink before you go.
I think I shall command your welcome here,
And, by all likelihood, some cheer is toward.

[*Knocks.*]

GREMIO [*coming forward*]
They're busy within; you were best knock louder.

PEDANT *looks out of the window.*

PEDANT [*as* VINCENTIO]
What's he that knocks as he would beat down the gate?

ACT 5, SCENE 1

Padua. The street in front of LUCENTIO's *house.* BIONDELLO, LUCENTIO, *and* BIANCA *enter;* GREMIO *precedes the rest and does not see the others.*

BIONDELLO
Go quietly and quickly, sir. The priest is ready.

LUCENTIO
I'll rush, Biondello. But they may need you at home. Therefore, leave us.

    Exits with BIANCA.

BIONDELLO
No, I'll see you safely to the church, and then go back to my "master's" as fast as I can. 5

    Exit.

GREMIO
I'm amazed that Cambio has not come yet.

    PETRUCHIO, KATE, VINCENTIO, GRUMIO, *and* ATTENDANTS *enter.*

PETRUCHIO
Sir, here's the door—this is Lucentio's house.
My father-in-law's house lies near the marketplace.
I must go there, so I'll leave you here, sir.

VINCENTIO
You must have a drink before you go. 10
I think I'll be able to guarantee your welcome here,
and it's likely that some entertainment will be available.

    Knocks.

GREMIO
They're busy inside. You'd better knock louder.

    PEDANT *looks out of the window.*

PEDANT, *as* VINCENTIO
Who's knocking there as if he'd beat down the door?

VINCENTIO

15   Is Signior Lucentio within, sir?

PEDANT [*as* VINCENTIO]

    He's within, sir, but not to be spoken withal.

VINCENTIO

    What if a man bring him a hundred pound or two to
    make merry withal?

PEDANT [*as* VINCENTIO]

    Keep your hundred pounds to yourself. He shall need
20   none, so long as I live.

PETRUCHIO [*to* VINCENTIO]

    Nay, I told you your son was well beloved in Padua.—Do
    you hear, sir? To leave **frivolous** circumstances, I pray you,
    tell Signior Lucentio that his father is come from Pisa and
    is here at the door to speak with him.

PEDANT [*as* VINCENTIO]

25   Thou liest. His father is come from Padua and is here
    looking out at the window.

VINCENTIO

    Art thou his father?

PEDANT [*as* VINCENTIO]

    Ay, sir, so his mother says, if I may believe her.

PETRUCHIO [*to* VINCENTIO]

    Why, how now, gentleman! Why, this is flat knavery, to
30   take upon you another man's name.

PEDANT [*as* VINCENTIO]

    Lay hands on the villain. I believe 'a means to cozen
    somebody in this city under my countenance.

       Reenter BIONDELLO.

BIONDELLO [*aside*]

    I have seen them in the church together. God send 'em
    good shipping! But who is here? Mine old master
35   Vincentio! Now we are undone and brought to nothing.

VINCENTIO

Is Signor Lucentio at home, sir? 15

PEDANT, *as* VINCENTIO

He's inside, sir, but you can't talk to him.

VINCENTIO

What if someone brought him a hundred or two hundred
pounds to entertain with?

PEDANT, *as* VINCENTIO

Keep your hundred pounds. He won't need any of that as
long as I'm alive. 20

PETRUCHIO

See, I told you that your son was well-loved in Padua. You see,
sir? (*to* PEDANT) To put aside trivial details, please tell Signor
Lucentio that his father has arrived from Pisa and is here
outside waiting to speak with him.

PEDANT, *as* VINCENTIO

You're lying! His father has arrived from Padua and is here 25
looking out the window.

VINCENTIO

Are you his father?

PEDANT, *as* VINCENTIO

Yes, sir, so his mother says—if I can believe her.

PETRUCHIO (*to* VINCENTIO)

Why, what's this, gentleman? Why, this is outright deception to
assume another man's name! 30

PEDANT, *as* VINCENTIO

Grab that liar! I think he intends to cheat somebody in this city
pretending he's me.

> BIONDELLO *enters.*

BIONDELLO (*aside*)

I saw them in the church together. God give them good luck!
But who's this here? My old master Vincentio! Now we're
done for, and our plan is ruined. 35

VINCENTIO [*seeing* BIONDELLO]
Come hither, crack-hemp.

BIONDELLO
I hope I may choose, sir.

VINCENTIO
Come hither, you rogue. What, have you forgot me?

BIONDELLO
Forgot you? No, sir. I could not forget you, for I never saw
you before in all my life.

VINCENTIO
What, you **notorious** villain, didst thou never see thy
master's father, Vincentio?

BIONDELLO
What, my old worshipful old master? Yes, marry, sir; see
where he looks out of the window.

VINCENTIO
Is 't so, indeed?

[*Beats* BIONDELLO.]

BIONDELLO
Help, help, help! Here's a madman will murder me.

[*Exit.*]

PEDANT [*as* VINCENTIO]
Help, son! Help, Signior Baptista!

[*Exits from above.*]

PETRUCHIO
Prithee, Kate, let's stand aside and see the end of this
controversy.

[*They retire.*]

Reenter PEDANT *with* SERVANTS, BAPTISTA, *and*
TRANIO [*as* LUCENTIO].

VINCENTIO (*seeing* BIONDELLO)

Come here, you gallows bird.

BIONDELLO

I hope I have some choice about that, sir.

VINCENTIO

Come here, you villain. Well? Have you forgotten me?

BIONDELLO

Forgotten you? No, sir. I can't forget you because I never saw
you before in my entire life. 40

VINCENTIO

What did you say, you outrageous villain! Have you never seen
your master's father, Vincentio, before?

BIONDELLO

What? My old dignified old master? Yes, indeed, sir—see him;
he's looking out the window.

VINCENTIO

Is that so? 45

He beats BIONDELLO.

BIONDELLO

Help, help, help! This madman here is trying to murder me.

Exit.

PEDANT, *as* VINCENTIO

Help, son! Help, Signor Baptista!

Leaves window.

PETRUCHIO

Come, Kate, let's stand over here and see how this argument
comes out.

They step aside.

PEDANT, BAPTISTA, TRANIO (*as* LUCENTIO), *and* SERVANTS
enter.

TRANIO [*as* LUCENTIO]

Sir, what are you that offer to beat my servant?

VINCENTIO

50   What am I, sir? Nay, what are you, sir? O immortal gods!
O fine villain! A silken doublet, a velvet hose, a scarlet
cloak, and a copatain hat! O, I am undone! I am undone!
While I play the good husband at home, my son and my
servant spend all at the university.

TRANIO [*as* LUCENTIO]

55   How now, what's the matter?

BAPTISTA

What, is the man lunatic?

TRANIO [*as* LUCENTIO]

Sir, you seem a sober ancient gentleman by your habit,
but your words show you a madman. Why, sir, what 'cerns
it you if I wear pearl and gold? I thank my good father, I

60   am able to maintain it.

VINCENTIO

Thy father! O villain, he is a sailmaker in Bergamo.

BAPTISTA

You mistake, sir, you mistake, sir! Pray, what do you think
is his name?

VINCENTIO

His name! As if I knew not his name! I have brought him

65   up ever since he was three years old, and his name is
Tranio.

PEDANT [*as* VINCENTIO]

Away, away, mad ass! His name is Lucentio, and he is
mine only son, and heir to the lands of me, Signior
Vincentio.

VINCENTIO

70   Lucentio! O, he hath murd'red his master! Lay hold on
him, I charge you, in the Duke's name. O, my son, my
son! Tell me, thou villain, where is my son Lucentio?

TRANIO, *as* LUCENTIO

Sir, who are you that you dare to beat my servant?

VINCENTIO

Who am I, sir! Well! Who are you, sir? Oh immortal gods! Oh   50
you well-dressed menial! Wearing a silken doublet! Velvet
breeches! A scarlet cloak! And a tall, cone-shaped hat! Oh, I've
been betrayed! I've been betrayed! While I act the careful
manager at home, my son and my servant spend everything
at the university!

TRANIO, *as* LUCENTIO

What's wrong? What's the matter?   55

BAPTISTA

Is the man mad?

TRANIO, *as* LUCENTIO

Sir, you seem to be a dignified old gentleman from your
manner, but you speak like a madman. Really, sir, why should it
concern you if I wear pearls and gold? Thanks to my good
father, I can afford it.   60

VINCENTIO

Your father! Oh you wretch! Your father is a sailmaker in
Bergamo.

BAPTISTA

You're mistaken, sir; you're really mistaken, sir. Just what do
you think his name is?

VINCENTIO

His name! As if I didn't know his name! I've raised him ever
since he was three years old! His name is Tranio!   65

PEDANT, *as* VINCENTIO

Go on, go on, you mad fool! His name is Lucentio, and he's my
only son and heir to my lands—the lands of Signor
Vincentio.

VINCENTIO

Lucentio! Oh, then he's murdered his master! Grab him, I order   70
you in the Duke's name. Oh my son, my son! Tell me, you wretch,
where's my son Lucentio?

TRANIO [*as* LUCENTIO]
Call forth an officer.

[*Enter one with an* OFFICER.]

Carry this mad knave to the gaol.—Father Baptista, I
75   charge you see that he be forthcoming.

VINCENTIO
Carry me to the gaol?

GREMIO
Stay, officer. He shall not go to prison.

BAPTISTA
Talk not, Signior Gremio; I say he shall go to prison.

GREMIO
Take heed, Signior Baptista, lest you be cony-catch'd in
80   this business. I dare swear this is the right Vincentio.

PEDANT [*as* VINCENTIO]
Swear, if thou dar'st.

GREMIO
Nay, I dare not swear it.

TRANIO [*as* LUCENTIO]
Then thou wert best say that I am not Lucentio.

GREMIO
Yes, I know thee to be Signior Lucentio.

BAPTISTA
85   Away with the **dotard**! To the gaol with him!

VINCENTIO
Thus strangers may be hal'd and abus'd.—O monstrous
villain!

Reenter BIONDELLO, *with* LUCENTIO *and* BIANCA.

BIONDELLO
O! We are spoil'd, and yonder he is! Deny him, forswear
him, or else we are all undone.

[*Exit* BIONDELLO, TRANIO, *and* PEDANT, *as fast as
may be.*]

TRANIO, *as* LUCENTIO

Call out an officer.

    An OFFICER *enters.*

Take this mad rascal to the jail. Father Baptista, I leave it to you
to see that he's available for trial.   75

VINCENTIO

Take me to jail?

GREMIO

Wait a minute, officer. You can't take him to prison.

BAPTISTA

Shut up, Signor Gremio. I say he will go to prison.

GREMIO

Beware, Signor Baptista, that you aren't tricked in this
business. I dare swear to you that this is the real Vincentio.   80

PEDANT, *as* VINCENTIO

Swear if you dare.

GREMIO

No, I don't dare swear it.

TRANIO, *as* LUCENTIO

Then maybe you'd dare say that I'm not Lucentio.

GREMIO

Yes, I know you're Signor Lucentio.

BAPTISTA

Take away that old fool. Take him to jail!   85

VINCENTIO

So, you let strangers be pestered and abused! Oh, you
monstrous villain!

    BIONDELLO, LUCENTIO, *and* BIANCA *enter.*

BIONDELLO

Oh, we're in for it! There he is—deny he is who he says he is,
refuse to recognize him, or else we'll all be caught.

    BIONDELLO, TRANIO, *and* PEDANT *exit very quickly.*

LUCENTIO [*kneeling*]

90   Pardon, sweet father.

VINCENTIO

                         Lives my sweet son?

BIANCA [*kneeling*]

     Pardon, dear father.

BAPTISTA

                    How hast thou offended?
     Where is Lucentio?

LUCENTIO

95   Here's Lucentio,
     Right son to the right Vincentio,
     That have by marriage made thy daughter mine
     While counterfeit supposes blear'd thine eyne.

GREMIO

     Here's packing, with a witness, to deceive us all!

VINCENTIO

100   Where is that damned villain Tranio,
     That fac'd and brav'd me in this matter so?

BAPTISTA

     Why, tell me, is not this my Cambio?

BIANCA

     Cambio is chang'd into Lucentio.

LUCENTIO

     Love wrought these miracles. Bianca's love
105   Made me exchange my state with Tranio,
     While he did bear my countenance in the town,
     And happily I have arriv'd at last
     Unto the wished haven of my bliss.
     What Tranio did, myself enforc'd him to;
110   Then pardon him, sweet father, for my sake.

VINCENTIO

     I'll slit the villain's nose that would have sent me to the
          gaol.

LUCENTIO (*Kneels.*)
Forgive me, my sweet father.   95

VINCENTIO
Is my sweet son alive?

BIANCA (*Kneels.*)
Forgive me, dear father.

BAPTISTA
What did you do wrong?
Where is Lucentio?

LUCENTIO
I'm Lucentio,   95
the real son to the real Vincentio,
who has made your daughter mine by marrying her
while pretenders fooled your eyes.

GREMIO
Here's scheming, blatant scheming, to fool everyone!

VINCENTIO
Where is that damned rascal Tranio,   100
who defied me and betrayed me in this business?

BAPTISTA
Why, tell me, isn't this my Cambio?

BIANCA
Cambio has changed into Lucentio.

LUCENTIO
Love has brought about these miracles. Bianca's love
has led me to change places with Tranio   105
while he played my part in the town.
And fortunately, I've at last reached
my desired paradise.
What Tranio did, I myself forced him to do.
So pardon him, sweet father, for my sake.   110

VINCENTIO
I'll slit the wretch's nose. He wanted to send me to jail.

BAPTISTA

But do you hear, sir? Have you married my daughter
without asking my goodwill?

VINCENTIO

115   Fear not, Baptista; we will content you. Go to! But I will in
to be reveng'd for this villainy.

    [*Exit.*]

BAPTISTA

And I, to sound the depth of this knavery.

    [*Exit.*]

LUCENTIO

Look not pale, Bianca; thy father will not frown.

    [*Exit* LUCENTIO *and* BIANCA.]

GREMIO

My cake is dough, but I'll in among the rest,
120   Out of hope of all but my share of the feast.

    [*Exit.*]

KATHERINE

Husband, let's follow, to see the end of this ado.

PETRUCHIO

First kiss me, Kate, and we will.

KATHERINE

What, in the midst of the street?

PETRUCHIO

What, art thou asham'd of me?

KATHERINE

125   No, sir, God forbid, but asham'd to kiss.

PETRUCHIO

Why, then let's home again. [*to* GRUMIO] Come, sirrah,
        let's away.

BAPTISTA

But did you hear, sir? Did you marry my daughter without asking my permission?

VINCENTIO

Don't worry, Baptista. We'll see that you're satisfied; don't get[115] upset. But I'll go inside and be revenged for this villainy.

Exits.

BAPTISTA

And I'll go in to get to the bottom of this scheming.

Exits.

LUCENTIO

Don't look pale, Bianca. Your father won't be upset.

LUCENTIO *and* BIANCA *exit.*

GREMIO

My plan has failed, but I'll join the others,
hoping now only for my share of the feast.   120

Exits.

KATHERINE

Husband, let's follow the others to see what happens.

PETRUCHIO

First give me a kiss, Kate, and then we will.

KATHERINE

What! In the middle of the street?

PETRUCHIO

What! Are you ashamed of me?

KATHERINE

No, sir, God forbid! Just ashamed to kiss.   125

PETRUCHIO

Well then, let's go home again.—Come, Grumio, let's go home.

KATHERINE

    Nay, I will give thee a kiss.   [*She kisses him.*]
                        Now pray thee, love, stay.

PETRUCHIO

130   Is not this well? Come, my sweet Kate.
    Better once than never, for never too late.

      [*Exeunt.*]

KATHERINE

    No, I'll give you a kiss. (*She kisses him.*) Now, please, my love,
        stay.

PETRUCHIO

    Isn't this better? Come, my sweet Kate.   130
    Better late than never, and never too late to mend.

    They exit.

ACT V, SCENE II

[*Padua. Lucentio's house.*] *Enter* BAPTISTA,
VINCENTIO, GREMIO, *the* PEDANT, LUCENTIO,
BIANCA, PETRUCHIO, KATHERINE, HORTENSIO
and WIDOW, TRANIO, BIONDELLO, *and* GRUMIO;
the SERVINGMEN *bringing in a banquet.*

LUCENTIO

At last, though long, our jarring notes agree,
And time it is, when raging war is done,
To smile at 'scapes and perils overblown.
My fair Bianca, bid my father welcome,
5   While I with selfsame kindness welcome thine.
Brother Petruchio, sister Katherina,
And thou, Hortensio, with thy loving widow,
Feast with the best, and welcome to my house.
My banquet is to close our stomachs* up
10   After our great good cheer. Pray you, sit down,
For now we sit to chat as well as eat.

PETRUCHIO

Nothing but sit and sit, and eat and eat!

BAPTISTA

Padua affords this kindness, son Petruchio.

PETRUCHIO

Padua affords nothing but what is kind.

HORTENSIO

15   For both our sakes, I would that word were true.

PETRUCHIO

Now, for my life, Hortensio fears* his widow!

WIDOW

Then never trust me if I be afeard.

PETRUCHIO

You are very sensible, and yet you miss my sense:
I mean, Hortensio is afeard of you.

---

9   *stomachs* Lucentio is punning on a second meaning of stomachs: "hot tempers."

16   *fears* means both "frightens" and "is frightened of"

ACT 5, SCENE 2

Padua, LUCENTIO'S *house.* BAPTISTA, VINCENTIO, GREMIO,
the PEDANT, LUCENTIO, BIANCA, PETRUCHIO, KATHERINE,
HORTENSIO *and* WIDOW, TRANIO, BIONDELLO, *and*
GRUMIO *all enter;* SERVINGMEN *enter with* TRANIO *and
bring in a dessert.*

LUCENTIO

At long last, we're all in accord,
and it's time, now that the heated war is finished,
to smile at past scrapes and dangers.
My lovely Bianca, welcome my father
while I, with equal kindness, welcome yours.   5
Brother Petruchio, sister Katherine,
and you, Hortensio, with your loving widow,
feast with the best of them and welcome to my house.
My dessert is to seal our stomachs
after our wonderful reception. Please, sit down.   10
Now we'll sit to talk as well as eat.

PETRUCHIO

Nothing except sitting and sitting, and eating and eating!

BAPTISTA

Padua is famous for this type of kindness, my son Petruchio.

PETRUCHIO

Padua offers nothing except what is kind.

HORTENSIO

For both of our sakes, I wish that were true.   15

PETRUCHIO

Well, I'd swear there's fear between Hortensio and his widow.

WIDOW

Never believe me again if I say I'm frightened.

PETRUCHIO

You're very sensible; and yet you misunderstood me:
I meant that Hortensio is frightened of you.

WIDOW

20   He that is giddy thinks the world turns round.

PETRUCHIO

        Roundly replied.

KATHERINE

                        Mistress, how mean you that?

WIDOW

        Thus I conceive by him.

PETRUCHIO

        Conceives by me? How likes Hortensio that?

HORTENSIO

25   My widow says, thus she conceives her tale.

PETRUCHIO

        Very well mended. Kiss him for that, good widow.

KATHERINE

        "He that is giddy thinks the world turns round"—
        I pray you, tell me what you meant by that.

WIDOW

        Your husband, being troubled with a shrew
30   Measures my husband's sorrow by his woe.
        And now you know my meaning.

KATHERINE

        A very mean meaning.

WIDOW

                        Right, I mean you.

KATHERINE

        And I am mean* indeed, respecting you.

PETRUCHIO

35   To her, Kate!

HORTENSIO

        To her, widow!

---

34   *mean* Kate is playing on another definition of mean: "gentle."

WIDOW
A dizzy man thinks the world is spinning. 20

PETRUCHIO
That's bluntly spoken.

KATHERINE
Madam, what do you mean by that?

WIDOW
Just what I conceived him to mean.

PETRUCHIO
Conceived by me! What do you think of that, Hortensio?

HORTENSIO
My widow said that she meant her statement as she said. 25

PETRUCHIO
Nicely explained. Kiss him for that, good widow.

KATHERINE
"A dizzy man thinks the world is spinning."
Please tell me what you meant by that.

WIDOW
Your husband, pestered by a shrew,
judges my husband's trouble to be his own trouble. 30
Now you know what I meant.

KATHERINE
A very mean meaning.

WIDOW
Exactly—I meant you.

KATHERINE
And I am gentle, indeed, compared with you.

PETRUCHIO
Get her, Kate! 35

HORTENSIO
Get her, widow!

PETRUCHIO

A hundred marks, my Kate does put her down.

HORTENSIO

That's my office.

PETRUCHIO

Spoke like an officer! Ha' to thee, lad.

[*Drinks to* HORTENSIO.]

BAPTISTA

40   How likes Gremio these quick-witted folks?

GREMIO

Believe me, sir, they butt together well.

BIANCA

Head and butt! An hasty-witted body
Would say your head and butt were head and horn.*

VINCENTIO

Ay, mistress bide, hath that awakened you?

BIANCA

45   Ay, but not frighted me. Therefore I'll sleep again.

PETRUCHIO

Nay, that you shall not; since you have begun,
Have at you for a bitter jest or two!

BIANCA

Am I your bird? I mean to shift my bush,
And then pursue me as you draw your bow.—
50   You are welcome all.

[*Exit* BIANCA, KATHERINE, *and* WIDOW.]

PETRUCHIO

She hath prevented me. Here, Signior Tranio,
This bird you aim'd at, though you hit her not.—
Therefore a health to all that shot and miss'd.

TRANIO

O, sir, Lucentio slipp'd me like his greyhound,
55   Which runs himself and catches for his master.

---

43   *horn* means both a "cuckold's horn" and "antlers to ram or butt"

PETRUCHIO
I'll bet a hundred marks that my Kate lays her out.

HORTENSIO
That's my job.

PETRUCHIO
Spoken like a dedicated worker. Here's to you, lad.

     Drinks to HORTENSIO.

BAPTISTA
How do you like these amusing people, Gremio?   40

GREMIO
Believe me, sir, they butt their heads together well.

BIANCA
Head and butt! A hasty person
might think your head and butt were head and horn.

VINCENTIO
So, madam bride, has that wakened you?

BIANCA
Yes, but not startled me, so I'll go to sleep again.   45

PETRUCHIO
Oh no you won't. Since you've started it,
watch out for a scalding joke or two.

BIANCA
So, I'm your prey? I'll change my perch, then,
and you can chase me as you're drawing your bow.
Everyone is welcome.   50

    BIANCA *exits with* KATHERINE *and* WIDOW.

PETRUCHIO
She's outfoxed me. Here, Signor Tranio:
you aimed at that quarry, though you didn't bag her—
therefore, a toast to everyone who shot and missed.

TRANIO
Oh sir! Lucentio unleashed me like his greyhound,
which runs and catches for his master.   55

PETRUCHIO

A good swift simile, but something currish.

TRANIO

'Tis well, sir, that you hunted for yourself;
'Tis thought your deer* does hold you at a bay.

BAPTISTA

O ho, Petruchio! Tranio hits you now.

LUCENTIO

60   I thank thee for that gird, good Tranio.

HORTENSIO

Confess, confess, hath he not hit you here?

PETRUCHIO

'A has a little **gall'd** me, I confess.
And, as the jest did glance away from me,
'Tis ten to one it maim'd you two outright.

BAPTISTA

65   Now, in good sadness, son Petruchio,
I think thou hast the veriest shrew of all.

PETRUCHIO

Well, I say no; and therefore, for assurance,
Let's each one send unto his wife,
And he whose wife is most obedient
70   To come at first when he doth send for her
Shall win the wager which we will propose.

HORTENSIO

Content. What is the wager?

LUCENTIO

                                              Twenty crowns.

PETRUCHIO

Twenty crowns!
75   I'll venture so much of my hawk or hound,
But twenty times so much upon my wife.

LUCENTIO

A hundred then.

---

58   *deer* means both a "doe" and a "dear one"

PETRUCHIO

A good, quick simile, but a little bit doggy.

TRANIO

It's a good thing that you hunt for yourself.
It's said that your deer has got you at a standoff.

BAPTISTA

Aha, Petruchio! Tranio got you there!

LUCENTIO

Thanks for that taunt, good Tranio.   60

HORTENSIO

Admit it, admit it! Didn't he get you with that one?

PETRUCHIO

He nicked me a little, I must admit.
And as the joke bounced away from me,
I'll bet ten to one that it hit you two squarely.

BAPTISTA

Now, in all seriousness, my son Petruchio,   65
I think you married the worst shrew of all.

PETRUCHIO

Well, I say I didn't. Therefore, to prove it,
let each one of us send for his wife.
The man whose wife is most obedient
and comes at once when he sends for her   70
will win the bet we agree on.

HORTENSIO

Agreed. What are the stakes?

LUCENTIO

Twenty crowns.

PETRUCHIO

Twenty crowns!
I'd chance that much on my hawk or hound   75
but twenty times that much upon my wife.

LUCENTIO

A hundred then.

HORTENSIO

                    Content.

PETRUCHIO

                         A match! 'Tis done.

HORTENSIO

80   Who shall begin?

LUCENTIO

    That will I.
    Go, Biondello, bid your mistress come to me.

BIONDELLO

    I go.

       [Exit.]

BAPTISTA

    Son, I'll be your half, Bianca comes.

LUCENTIO

85   I'll have no halves; I'll bear it all myself.

      Reenter BIONDELLO.

    How now, what news?

BIONDELLO

                    Sir, my mistress sends you word
    That she is busy, and she cannot come.

PETRUCHIO

    How? "She's busy and she cannot come"?
90   Is that an answer?

GREMIO

               Ay, and a kind one too.
    Pray God, sir, your wife send you not a worse.

PETRUCHIO

    I hope better.

HORTENSIO

    Sirrah Biondello, go and entreat my wife
95   To come to me forthwith.

      [Exit BIONDELLO.*]*

HORTENSIO
Agreed.

PETRUCHIO
It's a bet! Done.

HORTENSIO
Who should begin? 80

LUCENTIO
I will.
Go, Biondello, and tell your lady to come to me.

BIONDELLO
I'm going.

Exits.

BAPTISTA
Son, I'll cover half your bet that Bianca comes.

LUCENTIO
I won't bear just half. I'll take the whole bet. 85

BIONDELLO *enters.*

What's this? What happened?

BIONDELLO
Sir, my lady sends you a message
that she's busy and cannot come.

PETRUCHIO
What! "She's busy and cannot come!"
Is that a proper answer? 90

GREMIO
Yes, and a nice one, too.
You'd better pray, sir, that your wife doesn't send you a worse
one.

PETRUCHIO
I hope for a better one.

HORTENSIO
Servant Biondello, go and beg my wife
to come to me at once. 95

BIONDELLO *exits.*

PETRUCHIO

                   O, ho! Entreat her!
Nay, then, she must needs come.

HORTENSIO

                      I am afraid, sir,
Do what you can, yours will not be entreated.

    Reenter BIONDELLO.

100   Now, where's my wife?

BIONDELLO

She says you have some goodly jest in hand.
She will not come; she bids you come to her.

PETRUCHIO

Worse and worse; she will not come!
O vile, intolerable, not to be endur'd!—
105   Sirrah Grumio, go to your mistress,
Say, I command her come to me.

    [*Exit* GRUMIO.]

HORTENSIO

I know her answer.

PETRUCHIO

                What?

HORTENSIO

                   She will not.

PETRUCHIO

110   The fouler fortune mine, and there an end.

    Reenter KATHERINE.

BAPTISTA

Now by my holidam, here comes Katherine!

KATHERINE

What is your will, sir, that you send for me?

PETRUCHIO

Where is your sister, and Hortensio's wife?

KATHERINE

They sit conferring by the parlour fire.

PETRUCHIO
Oh ho! Beg her!
Well then, she has to come.

HORTENSIO
I'm afraid, sir,
that do whatever you like, your wife won't be begged.

　　　BIONDELLO *enters.*

Well, where's my wife? 　　　　　　　　　　　　　　　100

BIONDELLO
She says you're playing some kind of trick.
She won't come. She asks you to come to her.

PETRUCHIO
Worse and worse! She won't come! Oh terrible,
intolerable, not to be stood!
Servant Grumio, go to your lady. Tell her that 　　　105
I order her to come to me.

　　　GRUMIO *exits.*

HORTENSIO
I know what her answer will be.

PETRUCHIO
What?

HORTENSIO
She won't.

PETRUCHIO
My bad luck, then, and that will be an end to it. 　　　110

　　　KATHERINE *enters.*

BAPTISTA
Now, by a holy relic, here comes Katherine!

KATHERINE
What did you want, sir, when you asked me to come?

PETRUCHIO
Where's your sister and Hortensio's wife?

KATHERINE
They're sitting by the parlor fire and chatting.

PETRUCHIO

115   Go, fetch them hither. If they deny to come,
Swinge me them soundly forth unto their husbands.
Away, I say, and bring them hither straight.

      [*Exit* KATHERINE.]

LUCENTIO

Here is a wonder, if you talk of a wonder.

HORTENSIO

And so it is; I wonder what it bodes.

PETRUCHIO

120   Marry, peace it **bodes**, and love, and quiet life,
And awful rule, and right supremacy,
And, to be short, what not that's sweet and happy.

BAPTISTA

Now, fair befall thee, good Petruchio!
The wager thou hast won, and I will add
125   Unto their losses twenty thousand crowns,
Another dowry to another daughter,
For she is chang'd, as she had never been.

PETRUCHIO

Nay, I will win my wager better yet,
And show more sign of her obedience,
130   Her new-built virtue and obedience.

      Reenter KATHERINE, *with* BIANCA *and* WIDOW.

See where she comes and brings your froward wives
As prisoners to her womanly persuasion.—
Katherine, that cap of yours becomes you not;
Off with that bauble, throw it underfoot.

      [KATHERINE *throws down her cap.*]

WIDOW

135   Lord, let me never have cause to sigh
Till I be brought to such a silly pass!

BIANCA

Fie, what a foolish duty call you this?

PETRUCHIO

Go bring them here. If they refuse to come,   115
drive them to their husbands with a sound beating.
Go, I said, and bring them here at once.

      KATHERINE exits.

LUCENTIO

This is a wonder, if you speak of wonders.

HORTENSIO

Yes, it is. I wonder what it means.

PETRUCHIO

Really, it means peace, and love, and a quiet life,   120
a rule that will inspire respect and proper obedience.
In short, everything that's sweet and happy.

BAPTISTA

Well, good luck to you, good Petruchio!
You've won the bet, and I'll add
to their losses twenty thousand crowns—   125
another dowry for another daughter
because she has changed into someone totally different.

PETRUCHIO

Wait, I'll win my bet even more convincingly
and give you more proof of her obedience,
her new virtue and obedience.   130

      KATE, BIANCA, and WIDOW enter.

See, she's coming and bringing your stubborn wives
as prisoners of her gifts of womanly persuasion.
Katherine, that cap of yours doesn't become you—
take that bauble off; trample it.

      KATHERINE throws down her cap.

WIDOW

Lord! May I be spared all troubles   135
until I do such a silly thing!

BIANCA

How ridiculous! What kind of foolish obedience do you
    call that?

LUCENTIO

I would your duty were as foolish too.
The wisdom of your duty, fair Bianca,
140   Hath cost me a hundred crowns since suppertime.

BIANCA

The more fool you for laying on my duty.

PETRUCHIO

Katherine, I charge thee tell these headstrong women
What duty they do owe their lords and husbands.

WIDOW

Come, come, you're mocking; we will have no telling.

PETRUCHIO

145   Come on, I say, and first begin with her.

WIDOW

She shall not.

PETRUCHIO

I say she shall.— And first begin with her.

KATHERINE

Fie, fie! Unknit that threatening unkind brow,
And dart not scornful glances from those eyes
150   To wound thy lord, thy king, thy governor.
It blots thy beauty as frosts do bite the meads,
Confounds thy fame as whirlwinds shake fair buds,
And in no sense is meet or amiable.
A woman mov'd is like a fountain troubled,
155   Muddy, ill-seeming, thick, **bereft** of beauty,
And while it is so, none so dry or thirsty
Will deign to sip or touch one drop of it.
Thy husband is thy lord, thy life, thy keeper,
Thy head, thy sovereign, one that cares for thee,
160   And for thy maintenance commits his body
To painful labour both by sea and land,
To watch the night in storms, the day in cold,
Whilst thou liest warm at home, secure and safe,
And craves no other tribute at thy hands
165   But love, fair looks, and true obedience—

LUCENTIO

    I wish you were as foolish in your obedience, too.

    Your wise obedience, lovely Bianca,

    has cost me a hundred crowns since supper.   140

BIANCA

    You're an even bigger fool for betting on my obedience.

PETRUCHIO

    Katherine, I order you, tell these headstrong women

    what obedience you owe your lords and husbands.

WIDOW

    Come, come, you're mocking us. We won't have a lecture.

PETRUCHIO

    Come on, I said. Begin with her first.   145

WIDOW

    No she won't.

PETRUCHIO

    I say she will.—Begin with her first.

KATHERINE

    Shame, for shame! Stop scowling,

    and don't look with those scornful glances

    at your lord, your king, your ruler.   150

    It mars your beauty as frosts bite the flowers,

    spoils your reputation as tornadoes shake lovely buds,

    and is in no way proper or lovable.

    An angry woman is like a churning fountain:

    muddy, ugly, thick, stripped of beauty.   155

    And while it's like that, no one, no matter how parched and
        thirsty,

    will be willing to sip or touch one drop of it.

    Your husband is your lord, your life, your keeper,

    your ruler, your king. He's the one who will care for you,   160

    and to keep you in comfort, he dedicates himself

    to painful work, both by sea and land,

    keeping watch during stormy nights and during cold days

    while you're lying at home, safe and secure.

    And he doesn't ask any other favor from you

    except love, kind looks, and true obedience—   165

Too little payment for so great a debt.
Such duty as the subject owes the prince
Even such a woman oweth to her husband;
And when she is froward, **peevish**, sullen, sour,
170 And not obedient to his honest will,
What is she but a foul contending rebel
And graceless traitor to her loving lord?
I am asham'd that women are so simple
To offer war where thy should kneel for peace,
175 Or seek for rule, supremacy, and sway,
When they are bound to serve, love, and obey.
Why are our bodies soft and weak and smooth,
Unapt to toil and trouble in the world,
But that our soft conditions and our hearts
180 Should well agree with our external parts?
Come, come, you froward and unable worms!
My mind hath been as big as one of yours,
My heart as great, my reason haply more,
To **bandy** word for word and frown for frown;
185 But now I see our lances are but straws,
Our strength as weak, our weakness past compare,
That seeming to be most which we indeed least are.
Then vail your stomachs, for it is no boot,
And place your hands below your husband's foot;
190 In token of which duty, if he please,
My hand is ready, may it do him ease.

PETRUCHIO
Why, there's a wench! Come on, and kiss me, Kate.

[*They kiss.*]

LUCENTIO
Well, go thy ways, old lad, for thou shalt ha 't.

VINCENTIO
'Tis a good hearing when children are toward.

LUCENTIO
195 But a harsh hearing when women are froward.

too small a payment for such a large debt.
Such obedience as a subject owes to a prince,
just such obedience does a woman owe her husband.
And when she's stubborn, peevish, sullen, or sour
and does not obey his honorable will,   170
what is she except a disgusting rebel
and wicked traitor to her loving lord?
I'm ashamed that women are so foolish
as to fight when they should kneel to peace,
or seek leadership, dominance, and lordship   175
when they have sworn to serve, love, and obey.
Why are women's bodies so soft, weak, and smooth,
unsuited to work and laboring in the world,
unless our soft qualities and our tempers
should match our outer appearance?   180
Come, come, you willful and lowly worms!
My mind was as once as puffed up as yours,
my spirit as great, my reason perhaps greater,
to trade word for word and frown for frown.
But now I see our lances are just straws,   185
our strength as weak, our weakness beyond comparison,
that we try hardest to be that which we're least able to do.
So swallow your pride, because it's useless,
and put your hands beneath your husband's foot.
To symbolize my obedience, if he chooses to accept it,   190
my hand is ready if he chooses to use it.

PETRUCHIO

Why, that's a woman! Come on and kiss me, Kate.

They kiss.

LUCENTIO

Well, go on, old lad. You've won the bet.

VINCENTIO

It's pleasant news to hear that children are obedient.

LUCENTIO

But bad news when women are willful.   195

PETRUCHIO

Come, Kate, we'll to bed.

We three are married, but you two are sped.

[*to* LUCENTIO] 'Twas I won the wager, though you hit the
white,*

200   And being a winner, God give you good night!

[*Exit* PETRUCHIO *and* KATHERINE.]

HORTENSIO

Now, go thy ways, thou hast tam'd a curst shrew.

LUCENTIO

'Tis a wonder, by your leave, she will be tam'd so.

[*Exeunt.*]

---

199   *white* Petruchio means the "bull's-eye of a target" and "Bianca" (which means
"white" in Italian).

PETRUCHIO

Come, Kate, let's go to bed.

We three are married, but you two are done for.

(*to* LUCENTIO) I'm the one who won the bet, though you hit the
white.

So, being a winner, God give you a good night!   200

PETRUCHIO *and* KATE *exit.*

HORTENSIO

Well, go on. You've tamed a terrible shrew.

LUCENTIO

It's amazing, if you'll excuse me for saying so, that she has
been so tamed.

They exit.

Act V Review

Discussion Questions

1. What does Vincentio's reaction to Lucentio's and Tranio's deceptions reveal about his character?

2. Is Petruchio's request for a kiss in Scene i simply another test of Kate?

3. What does Petruchio mean when he remarks "Padua affords nothing but what is kind"?

4. How does Petruchio pursue an aim opposite to Lucentio's in the final scene?

5. How is suspense built up about the bet?

6. What is the essence of a wife's duty, according to Kate?

7. How has Kate's image changed over the course of the play? Explain whether you find it realistic.

8. How important are the servants in *The Taming of the Shrew*? Explain your answer using examples from the play.

Literary Elements

1. What is **ironic**, or unexpected, about the behavior of Bianca and the Widow at the wedding feast?

2. **Imagery** refers to word pictures that appeal to the five senses. Locate all the imagery related to animals in Act V, Scene ii, and explain what you think they are meant to suggest.

3. Name some of the **themes** addressed by events in the last act. From reading *The Taming of the Shrew*, what would you say Shakespeare believes about family conflicts and the courtship of young people?

4. A **symbol** represents something beyond its obvious meaning. Kate has this to say to other wives: "Place your hands below your husband's foot." What would such an action symbolize?

Writing Prompts

1. Prepare a rebuttal to Kate's conclusions about a woman's place.

2. Write another scene for the play that looks at the three couples after they have been married for ten years.

3. Write a final act in which Sly reappears to comment on the play and see the conclusion of the Lord's joke.

4. Write the lyrics to a song to be sung at the wedding feast in Act V. Try to narrate some of the events that preceded these marriages.

5. Write down Baptista's secret thoughts about his new sons-in-law. Which man do you think he prefers? Explain.

6. Write a capsule description of one of the play's minor characters, such as Baptista, Gremio, or Hortensio. What kind of person is each, and what quotations or actions from the play support your opinion? Write it all down.

7. Write a short scene in which you dramatize a conflict that Kate and Petruchio might have in their marriage. You might even want to include one of the minor characters from the play.

The Play in Review

Discussion Questions

1. Is Kate's statement at the end of the play about a woman's duties sincere or ironic? Discuss the reasons for your opinion.

2. Shakespeare seems to let Kate get the last word in the play, in her long monologue in Act V, Scene ii. What is Petruchio's reaction to her speech? Explain why you think Shakespeare ends the play like this.

3. Analyze Petruchio's character, and decide if he has any appealing characteristics. Do you think Kate genuinely loves him? Explain your opinion.

4. In the Induction to the play, the tinker Sly is asked to watch a play full of "mirth and merriment, / Which bars a thousand harms and lengthens life." Does this statement help us to understand *The Taming of the Shrew* any better? Explain your answer.

5. Now that you've finished reading the play, how do you think the subplot of Bianca's wooing contributes to the main story of the taming of Kate?

6. What seems to be the ideal of marriage as presented in the play?

7. Why do you think Shakespeare does not return to Christopher Sly and the plot that began *The Taming of the Shrew*? Consider what might be gained and what might be lost with such a conclusion.

Literary Elements

1. Shakespeare's highly descriptive language relies on **figurative language**—language that describes things by comparing them to something else. A **simile** makes a comparison between unlike things using the words *like* and *as* ("She sings as sweetly as a nightingale"). A **metaphor** makes a direct comparison between unlike things ("She is my house, my household stuff . . ."). Look for examples of similes and metaphors in *The Taming of the Shrew* and explain how you think these comparisons add to the drama and meaning of the play.

2. **Personification**—attributing human traits to nonhuman things or ideas—occurs in Act II, Scene i, when Tranio (as Lucentio) says to Gremio, "Graybeard, thy love doth freeze." Gremio responds, "But thine doth fry!" Of course, love is incapable of either freezing or frying; each man is insulting the other by mocking his foe's age. See if you can find other examples of personification in the play, and explain what you think they contribute.

3. In literature, **comedies** are typified by a lighthearted tone, achieved with verbal banter (puns, hyperbole, and other wordplay), farce, slapstick (physical comedy), disguises, and cross-dressing. Often in Shakespeare's comedies, young people must overcome their father's wishes in order to find true love; typically, the comedies end in marriage ceremonies. Citing specific examples from the play, show how many of these elements you recognize in *The Taming of the Shrew*.

4. **Irony** is the opposite of what might be expected; for example, it is ironic when Petruchio shows up at his own wedding dressed like a madman, asking "Where is my lovely bride?" The ending of *The Taming of the Shrew* contains many ironies. Name some examples and explain what makes them ironic.

Writing Prompts

1. In the 80s, a popular show called *Moonlighting* had a couple of main characters who—much like Kate and Petruchio—were always at each other's throats. In one episode, they even played the parts of Shakespeare's famous twosome. Think about a sitcom that features two people in love and at war with each other. Then write either a plot treatment—or summary—of it, or try your hand at writing a complete episode.

2. Research and write a paper on the Elizabethan concept of "wit."

3. Write a description of the character you find most appealing in the play. Summarize that character and provide quotations or actions from the play that say something about him or her.

4. View Franco Zeffirelli's 1966 film of *The Taming of the Shrew*, starring Richard Burton as Petruchio and Elizabeth Taylor as Kate. Both actors were at the height of their fame and legendary for their own tempestuous love affair. Watch the movie and write a review of it. Do you agree with the director's interpretation of Shakespeare's play? Make your opinion clear.

5. Investigate courtship and marriage customs and ceremonies during the Renaissance, and write an essay with examples.

Multimodal and Group Activities

1. Actors love Petruchio's passage in which he talks of "plain Kate and bonny Kate . . . " (Act II, Scene i). It is often used by them as a short monologue or dialogue for auditions. Find the passage, practice it, and deliver it to your group.

2. The famous battle of the sexes between Petruchio and Kate has been staged in as many different ways as there are directorial imaginations, from a sexy romp to a cruel farce. At times, Kate delivers her "submission speech" with hostility, at other times she appears as numb and brainwashed as a Stepford wife by this point of the play. In a famous Turkish production, a shawled Kate submits to her husband only after she has slit her veins; she then dies. With your classmates, think of an innovative way to stage the play's last scene. Think about how different settings, historical periods, cultures, and individual personalities can shape the words and lend new meanings to the play. Perform the scene for your class and compare different versions.

3. Debate the following:

   Resolved: Men are the natural authorities in a marriage.

   Resolved: Love at first sight is possible.

4. A storyboard is a layout of drawings used in moviemaking to show the sequence of shots in a scene. It looks a bit like a comic strip and is helpful for showing where to use close-ups, long-shots, and unusual camera angles. Select a scene from *The Taming of the Shrew* that you would like to see filmed, then create a storyboard showing what such a scene would look like.

5. With a classmate, assume the parts of Kate and Petruchio, and attend a marriage therapist with the goal of making your relationship work. A third person must play the part of the therapist. You may choose to ad lib (perform spontaneously) your session or prepare your lines in advance, detailing a specific conflict and the things leading up to it.

Shakespeare's Life

Many great authors can be imagined as living among the characters in their works. Historical records reveal how these writers spoke, felt, and thought. But Shakespeare is more mysterious. He never gave an interview or wrote an autobiography—not even one of his letters survives. What we know about his life can be told very briefly.

Shakespeare was born in April 1564. The exact date of his birth is unknown, but he was baptized on April 26 in the Stratford-upon-Avon church. His father, John, was a prominent local man who served as town chamberlain and mayor. Young William attended

grammar school in Stratford, where he would have learned Latin—a requirement for a professional career—and some Greek.

In 1582, William married Anne Hathaway. He was 18; she was 26. At the time of their marriage, Anne was already three months pregnant with their first daughter, Susanna. In 1585, the couple had twins, Judith and Hamnet. Hamnet died before reaching adulthood, leaving Shakespeare no male heir.

Even less is known about Shakespeare's life between 1585 and 1592. During that time, he moved to London and became an actor and playwright. He left his family behind in Stratford. Although he surely visited them occasionally, we have little evidence about what Shakespeare was like as a father and a husband.

Several of his early plays were written during this time, including *The Comedy of Errors*, *Titus Andronicus*, and the three parts of *Henry VI*. In those days, working in the theater was rather like acting in soap operas today—the results may be popular, but daytime series aren't recognized as serious art. In fact, many people were opposed to even allowing plays to be performed. Ministers warned their congregations of the dangers of going to plays.

But Shakespeare and his friends were lucky. Queen Elizabeth I loved plays. She protected acting companies from restrictive laws and gave them her permission to perform. Shakespeare wrote several plays to be performed for the queen, including *Twelfth Night*.

Queen Elizabeth I

After Elizabeth's death in 1603, Shakespeare's company became known as the King's Men. This group of actors performed for James I, who had ruled Scotland before becoming the King of England. Perhaps to thank James for his patronage, Shakespeare wrote *Macbeth*, which included two topics of strong interest to the King—Scottish royalty and witchcraft.

Unlike many theater people, Shakespeare actually earned a good living. By 1599, he was part owner of the Globe, one of the newest theaters in London. Such plays as *Othello*, *Hamlet*, and *King Lear* were first performed there.

In 1610 or 1611, Shakespeare moved back to the familiar surroundings of Stratford-upon-Avon. He was almost 50 years old, well past middle age by 17th-century standards. Over the years, he'd invested in property around Stratford, acquiring a comfortable estate and a family coat of arms.

But Shakespeare didn't give up writing. In 1611, his new play *The Tempest* was performed at court. In 1613, his play *Henry VIII* premiered. This performance was more dramatic than anyone expected. The stage directions called for a cannon to be fired when "King Henry" came on stage. The explosion set the stage on fire, and the entire theater burned to the ground.

Shakespeare died in 1616 at the age of 52. His gravestone carried this inscription:

> **Good friend for Jesus sake forbear**
> **To dig the dust enclosed here!**
> **Blest be the man that spares these stones,**
> **And curst be he that moves my bones.**

This little verse, so crude that it seems unlikely to be Shakespeare's, has intrigued countless scholars and biographers.

Anyone who loves Shakespeare's plays and poems wants to know more about their author. Was he a young man who loved Anne Whateley but was forced into a loveless marriage with another Anne? Did he teach school in Stratford, poach Sir Thomas Lucy's deer, or work for a lawyer in London? Who is the "dark lady" of his sonnets?

But perhaps we are fortunate in our ignorance. Orson Welles, who directed an all-black stage production of *Macbeth* in 1936, put it this way: "Luckily, we know almost nothing about Shakespeare . . . and that makes it so much easier to understand [his] works . . . It's an egocentric, romantic, 19th-century conception that the artist is more interesting and more important than his art."

In Shakespeare's world, there can be little question of which is truly important, the work or the author. Shakespeare brings up the curtain and then steps back into the wings, trusting the play to a cast of characters so stunningly vivid that they sometimes seem more real than life.

Shakespeare's Theater

In Shakespeare's London, a day's entertainment often began with a favorite amusement, bearbaiting. A bear would be captured and chained to a stake inside a pit. A pack of dogs would be released, and they would attack the bear. Spectators placed bets on which would die first. Admission to these pits cost only a penny, so they were very popular with working-class Londoners.

The Swan Theatre in London, drawn in 1596, the only known contemporary image of an Elizabethan theater interior

After the bearbaiting was over, another penny purchased admission to a play. Each theater had its own company of actors, often supported by a nobleman or a member of the royal family. For part of his career, Shakespeare was a member of the Lord

Chamberlain's Men. After the death of Queen Elizabeth I, King James I became the patron of Shakespeare's company. The actors became known as the King's Men.

As part owner of the Globe Theatre, Shakespeare wrote plays, hired actors, and paid the bills. Since the Globe presented a new play every three weeks, Shakespeare and his actors had little time to rehearse or polish their productions. To complicate matters even more, most actors played more than one part in a play.

Boys played all the female roles. Most acting companies had three or four youths who were practically raised in the theater. They started acting as early as age seven and played female roles until they began shaving. Shakespeare had a favorite boy actor (probably named John Rice) who played Cleopatra and Lady

Richard Tarleton, Elizabethan actor famous for his clowning

Macbeth. Actresses would not become part of the English theater for another fifty years.

The audience crowded into the theater at about 2 p.m. The cheapest seats weren't seats at all but standing room in front of the stage. This area, known as the "pit," was occupied by "groundlings" or "penny knaves," who could be more trouble to the actors than they were worth. If the play was boring, the groundlings would throw rotten eggs or vegetables. They talked loudly to their friends, played cards, and even picked fights with each other. One theater was set on fire by audience members who didn't like the play.

The theater was open to the sky, so rain or snow presented a problem. However, the actors were partially protected by a roof known as the "heavens," and wealthier patrons sat in three stories of sheltered galleries that surrounded the pit and most of the main stage.

The main stage, about 25 feet deep and 45 feet wide, projected into the audience, so spectators were closely involved in the action. This stage was rather bare, with only a few pieces of furniture. But this simplicity allowed for flexible and fluid staging. Unlike too many later productions, plays at the Globe did not grind to a halt for scene changes. When one group of actors exited through one doorway and a new group entered through another, Shakespeare's audience understood that a new location was probably being represented.

Behind the main stage was the "tiring-house," where the actors changed costumes. Above the stage was a gallery that, when it wasn't occupied by musicians or wealthy patrons, could suggest any kind of high place—castle ramparts, a cliff, or a balcony.

Special effects were common. A trap door in the main stage allowed ghosts to appear. Even more spectacularly, supernatural beings could be lowered from above the stage. For added realism, actors hid bags of pig's blood and guts under their stage doublets. When pierced with a sword, the bags spilled out over the stage and produced a gory effect.

All these staging methods and design elements greatly appealed to Elizabethan audiences and made plays increasingly popular. By the time Shakespeare died in 1616, there were more than thirty theaters in and around London.

What would Shakespeare, so accustomed to the rough-and-tumble stagecraft of the Globe, think of the theaters where his plays are performed today? He would probably miss some of the vitality of the Globe. For centuries now, his plays have been most often performed on stages with a frame called the "proscenium arch," which cleanly separates the audience from the performers. This barrier tends to cast a peculiar shroud of privacy over his plays so that his characters do not seem to quite enter our world.

But with greater and greater frequency, Shakespeare's plays are being performed out-of-doors or in theaters with three- or four-sided stages. And a replica of the Globe Theatre itself opened in London in 1996, only about 200 yards from the site of the original.

The new Globe Theatre, London

This new Globe is an exciting laboratory where directors and actors can test ideas about Elizabethan staging. Their experiments may change our ideas about how Shakespeare's plays were performed and give new insights into their meaning.

The Globe Theatre

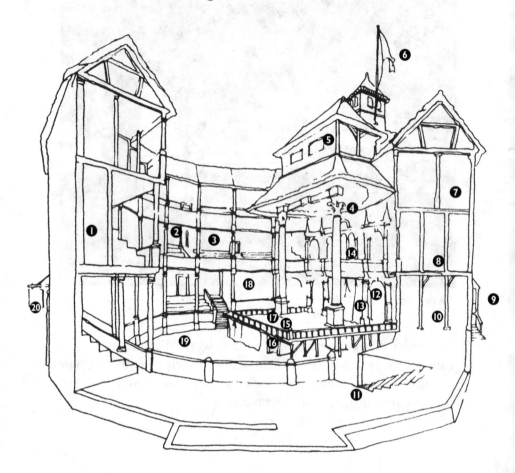

1 **Corridor** A passageway serving the middle gallery.

2 **Entrance** Point leading to the staircase and upper galleries.

3 **Middle Gallery** The seats here were higher priced.

4 **The Heavens** So identified by being painted with the zodiac signs.

5 **Hut** A storage area that also held a winch system for lowering characters to the stage.

6 **Flag** A white flag above the theater meant a show that day.

7 **Wardrobe** A storage area for costumes and props.

8 **Dressing Rooms** Rooms where actors were "attired" and awaited their cues.

9 **Tiring-House Door** The rear entrance or "stage door" for actors or privileged spectators.

10 **Tiring-House** Backstage area providing space for storage and costume changes.

11 **Stairs** Theatergoers reached the galleries by staircases enclosed by stairwells.

12 **Stage Doors** Doors opening into the Tiring-House.

13 **Inner Stage** A recessed playing area, often curtained off except as needed.

14 **Gallery** Located above the stage to house musicians or spectators.

15 **Trap Door** Leading to the Hell area, where a winch elevator was located.

16 **Hell** The area under the stage, used for ghostly comings and goings or for storage.

17 **Stage** Major playing area jutting into the Pit, creating a sense of intimacy.

18 **Lords Rooms** or private galleries. Six pennies let a viewer sit here, or sometimes on stage.

19 **The Pit** Sometimes referred to as "The Yard," where the "groundlings" watched.

20 **Main Entrance** Here the doorkeeper collected admission.

IMAGE CREDITS

www.clipart.com: 4, 7, 9, 11, 288, 290, 291; Library of Congress: 5, 8, 287;
© George E. Joseph: 6, 171, 240; © John Springer Collection/CORBIS: 16;
Donald Cooper/Photostage: 19, 93, 135, 168; Photofest: 90;
COLUMBIA/ KOBAL COLLECTION: 132; ©Bettmann/CORBIS: 243;
© Pawel Libera/CORBIS: 293

Every reasonable effort has been made to properly acknowledge ownership of all material used. Any omissions or mistakes are not intentional and, if brought to the publisher's attention, will be corrected in future editions.